MW00444866

THIS BOOK BELONGS TO:

PRAISE FOR *COZY WHITE COTTAGE*

"As a longtime fan of Liz Marie's, it's pure pleasure to sit and devour every unique detail of her charming White Cottage Farm in one beautiful book. Reading *Cozy White Cottage*, I felt like I was sitting across the table and sharing a cup of coffee with a good friend—a friend who just happens to have some of the best decorating tips and DIY ideas for creating a personal and inviting home. My copy is tagged with more than a few sticky notes!"

—**JENNIFER KOPF**, HOMES EDITOR, *COUNTRY LIVING* MAGAZINE

"The space we come home to should be filled with beauty, passion, and peace. In her book, *Cozy White Cottage*, Liz leaves no detail to chance—from furnishing each room to the soft glow of the light bulb we choose. Designing your home, 'the Liz way' will make you feel like you just got a big hug every time you walk through your door."

—**KIM LEGGETT**, AUTHOR, *CITY FARMHOUSE STYLE*

"All the cozy feelings! Whatever your personal home style might be, I believe it should start with cozy, peaceful, welcoming vibes, and that's just what Liz's book provides: the ultimate guide to styling a cozy home for your favorite people! Honored to be included in these beautiful pages!"

—BLOGGER **ERIN KERN** OF @COTTONSTEM
INSTAGRAM AND WWW.COTTONSTEM.COM

We cannot say enough about how much we love Liz Marie's approach to beautiful and inviting spaces. Her talent for creating places that feel cozy, lived in, and loved in is something we deeply admire and are in complete awe of. This book feels like a direct line into her heart and soul and we are so grateful that she has chosen to share it with us all!

—**ANDY AND CANDIS MEREDITH**, AUTHORS, *OLD HOME LOVE*

COZY *white* COTTAGE

100 WAYS TO LOVE
THE FEELING OF BEING HOME

LIZ MARIE
· GALVAN ·

PHOTOGRAPHY BY ANNA VANDERBERG

THOMAS NELSON
Since 1798

Cozy White Cottage

© 2019 by Liz Marie Galvan

All rights reserved. No portion of this book may be reproduced, stored in a retrieval system, or transmitted in any form or by any means—electronic, mechanical, photocopy, recording, scanning, or other—except for brief quotations in critical reviews or articles, without the prior written permission of the publisher.

Published in Nashville, Tennessee, by Thomas Nelson. Thomas Nelson is a registered trademark of HarperCollins Christian Publishing, Inc.

Photography by Anna Vanderberg

Thomas Nelson titles may be purchased in bulk for educational, business, fund-raising, or sales promotional use. For information, please email SpecialMarkets@ThomasNelson.com.

Any Internet addresses, phone numbers, or company or product information printed in this book are offered as a resource and are not intended in any way to be or to imply an endorsement by Thomas Nelson, nor does Thomas Nelson vouch for the existence, content, or services of these sites, phone numbers, companies, or products beyond the life of this book.

ISBN-13: 978-1-4003-1532-1

Printed in China

19 20 21 22 23 DSC 10 9 8 7 6 5 4 3

*To my grandma, who has always inspired and encouraged
my love for home décor and creating a cozy home.
And to Jose and Cope, whose love makes my life cozier than I ever dreamed.*

CONTENTS

INTRODUCTION

ozy. It's a word that just instantly makes you want to curl up by the fire with a blanket and some hot cocoa and snuggle with a good book, right? For some, coziness is the scent of a candle burning and the familiar taste of your mom's signature meal. For others, it's the sound of waves crashing, the cuddle of a beloved pet, or the sight of a sunset on the mountains. Maybe your version of cozy is something else entirely. You see, *cozy* can mean so many different things to different people.

Comfort, warmth, security . . . for me, these three things evoke coziness—that soul-deep feeling of being at home. As a girl growing up in Michigan, I felt most at home when I was doing something related to art, design, and decorating. I was drawn to decorating magazines and TV shows, which was a little unusual for a 14-year-old. After growing up and marrying an active-duty military service member, I was quickly thrown out of my comfort zone. My husband, Jose, and I were relocated to North Carolina, surrounded by strangers from different walks of life, and the one and only familiar thing I knew (Jose) would leave for more than six months at a time.

If comfort, warmth, and security were my pillars of coziness, I had lost two of the three. Being stationed in North Carolina, at least I had *warmth*, but even that had its limitations. To feel more at home, I needed to find the missing pillars, and that was when I began focusing much of my time on interior design. Creating cozy spaces in our rented townhouse helped keep my mind at ease instead of worried about a deployed husband and best friends many miles away. Trying my hand at DIY projects and incorporating some

cottage style into that rental brought me so much joy and added subtle hints of home, a way to find comfort in an unfamiliar place.

Since that time, Jose and I have taken on home projects of all different shapes and sizes, learning to keep up a house and taking on the easy repairs, décor refreshes, and DIY projects to make it better—to make it cozy. Through the years we've shared what we've learned on LizMarieBlog.com in hopes of helping others with tutorials, crafts, ways to incorporate cottage and farmhouse style, and simple inspiration. We have also opened up our hearts and lives with our wonderful readers. From the hardships of military life, to receiving the incredible gift of our son Copeland Beau, and to many hardships in between, life hasn't been perfect, but it's been a beautiful journey I've enjoyed sharing on the blog.

Through it all, one thing I am still dependent on is a cozy space to decompress and relax. Jose and I now find cozy in Michigan, on the eight acres we call White Cottage Farm. We are slowly turning this centennial property into our own as we renovate its 1800s farmhouse and add some special animals to the mix. At the moment, the farm is home to six sheep, three dogs, seven cats, twelve chickens, and approximately 100,000 bees. It is ever growing and ever blooming, and we are thankful every day for the peace and comfort our haven brings us. Jose and I lead such busy lives between the farm, our fixer-upper farmhouse, the boutique of vintage finds and home décor called The Found Cottage that we co-own, and other avenues of craziness, so having an oasis to come home to and shut out the rest of the world means so much to us.

Isn't *that* the importance of home? Although we all might define *cozy* differently, each definition offers the same promise: a sense of belonging, comfort, and warmth. A corner, a room, a place where our souls find peace and our bodies can rest. And although the craziness of life might tell us we don't have the time or energy to create a cozy home, I'm here to tell you that it's totally within reach.

Some may ask, "Why were you ready to write a book now?" My answer: I'm not. There's never a perfect time—and it's especially not ideal while our fixer-upper has no finished parts to it! But I hope through this book and a glimpse into our unfinished and imperfect life, you see that you can make your home cozy no matter what your life looks like right now.

It is my hope that *Cozy White Cottage* will inspire you to bring cozy into the way you live *today*, whether it's on a sheep-filled farm, in a modern urban flat, or in a rented townhouse. Wherever you are, let these tips and ideas help you create a sanctuary you and your family can gather in, live in, and love in. May these one hundred ways for adding comfort and warmth truly help you create a cozy corner of the world that you long to come home to.

WELCOME

PORCH & ENTRYWAY

A cozy place for warm greetings

PORCH & ENTRYWAY

What is it about some houses that beckons you to enter? Is it flowers on the porch? Flickering gaslights and a wreath on the door? An entryway that immediately offers a place to land and a neck to hug? So many elements play into a sense of hospitality and welcome. If we want to make our homes cozy, it all starts here where our guests and our families enter.

The porch and entryway become a sort of microcosm of the interior world they announce—the sights, the sounds, and the scents that make your home *yours*. When guests are greeted by the perfect soft rug, the sound of laughter from the kitchen, and your favorite cinnamon spice candle, they immediately sense your unique definition of home. Without saying a word, these elements offer a clear and cozy message: "You are welcome here—come on in."

№
01

A MARKET-
BAG GREETING

Wreaths on a door offer a cozy welcome, but what if you could really amp that coziness up by creating a unique door decoration with interchangeable stems and florals? I've been hanging a market bag on our front door for some time now, filling it with seasonal greens or flowers. I love the unique cottage vibe it adds to our entrance. The best part is it requires very little effort to change out the stems each season. It's instant cozy cottage charm to make your guests feel welcome.

Here are some of my favorite seasonal stems and blossoms to fill a market bag:

FALL: bittersweet and colorful leafy tree branches

WINTER: holly branches and pine boughs

SPRING: flowering tree branches or tulips (place the pots from the nursery right inside the bag!)

SUMMER: ferns or hydrangeas (again, you can use small nursery pots, or place cut stems in a tall plastic vase or bottle)

№ 02

TERRACOTTA POTS

A lot of people seem to think they should have a complete vision for their home's design before they even start. But please hear me: I typically dive in without a complete plan for how I want the entire room to look. Instead I add a little something here . . . I move a little something there. I find things I gravitate toward, and later I might reflect on how the room came together.

This is how I one day realized that I had been turning sections of my home into a greenhouse. Our sunroom is a perfect example. I hadn't planned on it being filled with lavender and rosemary topiaries or messy, sprawling plants like lemon thyme. But those are what I gravitated toward, so those are what now fill the room. They bring pops of color into the space, as well as some soothing and refreshing smells. But the abundance of cool greens does need to be balanced with some warm earth tones, and the easiest

way to do so is with the very pots the plants are housed in.

Terracotta pots are the most timeless keeper of our garden herbs and flowers. The color and feel take us back to the earth itself. If you want your cottage-inspired look to toe the line with an English greenhouse, bring as much of the greenhouse inside as you can, starting with the terracotta pots.

When incorporating these lovelies into your décor, gather a variety of shapes, sizes, and colors. Place them together in small corners to bring texture, scale, and light to any space that seems "lost" and could use a nice dose of earthy charm. Take the charm even further by pairing some of the pots with stoneware or vintage plates rather than the traditional drainage saucers.

When setting up the vignette, keep a few things in mind. First, watch the overall scale and silhouette of the grouping

6

to keep it in perspective. Since terracotta pots, as well as the plants inside, are often narrow and vertical, use enough pots to widen the grouping's overall stance and make it proportionate to the height.

Next, balance. It's best to mimic the asymmetrical beauty found in nature, so balance the vignette by ensuring its weight flows easily from one side to the other. Watch for any forced displays of ascension. So instead of making the silhouette look like a staircase (nature doesn't usually work that way), aim for a complex mountain range.

Last, add some empty terracotta pots to the vignette too. Keeping them bare not only draws special attention to unique pots in your collection, but it also conveys a message of future growth. After all, pot collections, plants, design plans—they all need a little room to grow!

DIY:

HOW TO BUILD BOX PLANTERS

Funny how we often flank our front doors with plants to greet our next visitors. I suppose if you can't have a plate of warm cookies waiting outside the door for them, at least you can have a beautiful plant! It does seem to signal that "this house is filled with beauty and life."

If the cost of large-scale planters to hold your welcome plants is daunting, try making your own! Here's what you'll need:

ITEMS NEEDED:

Tools

Miter saw

Table saw

Pneumatic nail gun

Tape measure

Wood filler

Sand paper

Paint

MATERIALS:

Four 2" x 2" x 6' pine (legs)

Eight 1" x 6" x 6' pine (side panels)

Two 2" x 4" x 6' pine (top trim)

One 1/2" x 2' x 4' sanded plywood (bottom board)

① Use the 2" x 2" x 6' boards for the legs. Cut them to 22$\frac{1}{2}$ inches using the miter saw.

② The 1" x 6" x 6' boards are going to be used to make the side panels or horizontal pieces between the legs. Cut all the 1" x 6" to 15 inches long. Take four of the (now) 1" x 6" x 15" and rip them on the table saw to 1" x 3 3/4" x 15". These are going to be used for the top board of each face of the panels.

③ Nail the legs to the side panel boards, starting from the top and working your way down. Repeat this step to the other adjacent panels until you have all sides complete.

④ Once all side panels are attached to the legs, attach all panels and legs together to create the box.

⑤ Next cut the 2" x 4" x 6' top trim boards at 45-degree angles. The long edge of the top trim board measures at 19 ½ inches. Cut four boards at the same measurement. Place them on top, matching up the 45-degree angle cuts. Center the top trim boards on the lower portion of the planter box, and nail it into place.

⑥ The bottom board is plywood cut 15" x 15", notching out the inside corners of the legs, nailed across the bottom face of the panels. If heavy plants are going to be used, use a scrap piece of the legs in the center of the bottom board for added support.

⑦ For a clean look, fill all the holes and indents from the nail gun with wood filler, and sand before painting. Once all is done, the real fun can start: painting!

№ 04 ADD HISTORICAL CHARM

There's just something about a historical home with all its architectural details and aged beauty that automatically oozes coziness. Honestly, it's so effortless when designing a room with lots of historical detail because the room tends to speak for itself. Aged beadboard walls, chippy corbels, authentic shiplap, large chunky trim, exposed brick, and tin ceilings—all demand attention in a space and make decorating easy because the historical details do all the hard work.

But what happens when you move into a new home but still crave those yummy historical details that make the home tell more of a story and add that texture and dimension that only those details can add? Here are a few quick tips to add some historical detail to any home:

- Add some chippy corbels to places that make sense in your home, like an archway or brackets for shelving or a DIY mantle.
- Add historical wall treatments such as beadboard, shiplap, brick, vintage-inspired wallpaper, and gorgeous antique-inspired molding for instant old-home charm.
- Find sellers of salvaged items such as brick, lights, doors, shiplap, barnwood, and other items that you could use to renovate your home or build around if you are dealing with new construction. Many times you can find places in your area that are selling large lots of these items so you can use them throughout your home.
- Use antique interior doors rather than new doors. They just don't make doors like they used to with all the gorgeous detail, and an old door can take your home from builder grade to custom in no time.

Sometimes simply using vintage and antique pieces, from art to furniture, can be the perfect historical touch. Antique and vintage inspired sofas are readily available, and I find the best home décor at flea markets and antique shops from architectural salvage, vintage art, primitive cabinets, and more that add to the historical charm of our home.

11

N° 05

WOOD AND WHITE

As I think back to my early days of decorating, it kind of scares me. I cringe as I look at old photos and wonder why I ever thought any of that looked good. But something tells me there will always be things about our earlier décor that we question as time goes on. One thing that has remained the same in my décor no matter how much my style has changed is my love for wood and white. What is wood and white, you ask? Just the simple combination of wood tones mixed with white paint. One of the first times I intentionally combined the two was when I painted a coffee table's legs white and left the top wood. I'm in no way saying I invented this combination, far from it, but I realized very early the warmth and coziness this combination can give a room.

Want to know one of my favorite parts about the wood-and-white combination? The non-commitment. If you follow my blog and have for some time now, you

realize how much I change things around in our house. It's a habit I think will forever be a part of me, but the wood-and-white combination on a single piece of furniture like a coffee table or a dresser is a commitment to neither the wood nor the white; it's marrying the two together to bring interest and detail to the space.

A great lesson I learned early on with my love for white walls and white décor is that if a room doesn't feel anchored or seems too cold, add some wood tones to warm up the space. Placing a large wood armoire, a wood coffee table, or some wood accents next to a white sofa can make a world of difference.

Now, if the thought of painting a wood piece grips your heart with fear, start small. Leave your grandmother's priceless antique buffet alone. Instead, keep your eyes open at garage sales and on Craigslist for some well-made but affordable wood furniture. A second-hand dresser, bedside

table, end table, or coffee table offer a perfect opportunity for giving the wood-and-white combo a try.

To create a wood-and-white piece, start with an all-wood piece and simply choose what parts you want to leave as is and what parts you want to paint white. Let's say you have a dresser and choose to paint the shell of the piece white and keep the drawers wood. Take the drawers out of the piece. Paint the entire shell of the dresser white and distress with sandpaper if you want a chippy look. For the drawers, you can sand any damaged areas on the wood and apply a wood oil such as hemp oil to refresh the surfaces. When it's all dry, put the drawers back in the dresser, and you have the perfect wood-and-white piece. Find a special spot for your new piece, and style with a mirror, plant, and a charming little lamp.

Wood and white isn't limited to just furniture; it can be used in décor in every room of your home. Imagine a white chippy table with wood candleholders on it, or a room with all white walls and white sofas with a gorgeous wooden armoire to anchor the room as the focal point. The wood-and-white combo can be your go-to for any style home—from cottage to farmhouse. So now you know the secret: wood and white are the best of friends. The combo is classic, it's timeless, and it's a secret ingredient to cozy.

FAVORITE COZY BASICS

Start with these cozy basics in any space, and soon you'll be all set in a place of cozy contentment with no other changes needed.

🌾 **Add a rug.** Choose a natural fiber rug alone or layered under a patterned cozy wool rug. A jute rug is both easy to clean and the perfect base for any cozy space.

🌾 **Use white paint.** Paint your walls a cozy fresh warm white such as Benjamin Moore White Dove. I love White Dove because it offers that fresh white with warm undertones.

🌾 **Paint a piece of furniture.** I love to have at least one painted piece of furniture in every room to add character. I prefer authentically old chippy white paint, but if I can't find that and need to do the job myself, my go-to paint color is Raw Silk by Fusion Mineral Paint.

🌾 **Add wood tones.** A wooden piece of furniture or an accent piece is important in every space. A wooden frame, a wooden blanket ladder, or a wooden armoire can up a room's cozy factor. Always add some natural wood grain to every space.

- **Incorporate plants.** Every space needs a little green. My favorite cozy plant is a topiary, whether it's angel vine or rosemary in a worn, rustic pot on a coffee table, in a centerpiece, on a dresser, on a mantle, or anywhere that needs a little life added.
- **Load up on texture.** Knit pillows and throws tossed on a sofa, chair, or bench amp up the cozy factor instantly.
- **Add something shiny.** A mirror or even some metal candlesticks instantly add a hint of elegance to your space that makes your eyes want to linger longer.

BINGO

3	16	40	58	75
14	30	42	55	67
	23	FREE	50	69

ANTIQUES

THE HOUSE THAT PINTEREST BUILT   DIANE KEATON

N° 07

MY TOP TEN ITEMS TO PICK UP WHILE ANTIQUING

1. **Antique books.** Antique books are a great thing to have lying around because you can never have too many! They are great for styling bookshelves, coffee tables, entryway tables, nightstands, and so much more.

2. **Baskets.** You can find some amazing baskets, from metal to wicker, while you are out antiquing. I love using wicker baskets to hold quilts and greenery or to display on shelves.

3. **Stoneware dishes.** I think stoneware dishes are a classic item to collect. I love using stoneware dishes in displays in our kitchen and dining room, but we also use our antique stoneware as our everyday dishes as well!

4. **Scales.** Scales come in so many great different shapes, sizes, and colors. Use scales on shelves, in the kitchen, to style tables, and so much more. I love the uniqueness of antique scales and the unique element they add to a vignette.

5. **Corbels.** If you follow me on my blog or social media, you know that one of my biggest obsessions is corbels. Especially if they are white and chippy. I use them as shelf brackets, in vignettes, and styled on shelves.

6. **Antique stools.** I love using antique stools in our home because of the charm they bring that a new stool can't always offer. Sporting chippy paint or gorgeous worn wood, they get to work adding seating everywhere from a desk to the kitchen island. For those amazing stool finds that aren't as sturdy, I love using them as plant stands to cozy up corners of our home and add some rustic texture and greenery.

7. **Vintage paper.** When I see vintage science posters, vintage pages out of bird or garden books, and other vintage paper

products that go with our home and décor, I love picking them up for future projects like framing for gallery walls or wrapping gifts. I also love to clip them on antique clipboards and hang them up.

8. **Antique doors.** One of my dreams was to find antique doors to replace all the new doors in our home and add tons of charm and architecture to all our spaces. You can find amazing antique doors at flea markets, antique shops, and salvage yards to fit your doorways and style. Hang them with hinges like a normal door, or use barn-door hardware to hang them for closet doors, laundry room doors, and so much more.

9. **Vintage pottery.** This is a favorite pick up of mine because of my love for houseplants. Vintage pottery in different colors, shapes, designs, and textures are great for so many things from simply displaying on shelves to replacing normal houseplant pots and storing trinkets. Once you start collecting vintage pottery, be warned that it might be hard to stop.

10. **Architectural salvage and art.** In our home, you can find architectural salvage and art hanging all over the walls, from windows and corbels to vintage portraits and antique framed art. They are packed with charm and add instant coziness to a space.

№ 08

MAKE A MOOD BOARD

One mistake I make in many areas of my life is overdoing it. I order too much at a restaurant because it all sounds delicious. I over spend at the grocery store because I shop while I'm hungry. And I overbuy when I purchase items to decorate a room if I don't go in with a plan. So it's best that I organize my thoughts and plans for the space *before* I open my wallet. To do that, I use a mood board.

Mood boards are places to collect and curate a visual reference for your space—colors, fabrics, textures, ideas, and pieces of inspiration. I started making them in interior design school, well, actually before then with my former love for scrapbooking. I would clip magazine images and glue them in a book. That was pre-Pinterest or PP as I like to call it (a weird time), but it still got the job done. At a glance I could see the styles, colors, and patterns that were catching my eye.

A mood board sets the tone for a room. If you want to make your own, it can range from creating a design collage on a website or with design software to curating a Pinterest board. You could even use an actual board if you want to include physical fabric samples, photos, or sketches. Gather all the elements in one place—from paint colors to lighting to furniture to accessories. It's amazing what pulling it all together can do for your time, budget, and even your sanity. A mood board really helps you organize your thoughts *before* you start on your big project. You'll be much less likely to overdo it while shopping, and you'll also end up with a space that's full of inspiration.

N⁰ 09   REDUCE, REUSE, REPURPOSE

At times this whole decorating thing can seem overwhelming in so many ways, but one of the biggest ways is with your budget. You might be staring at a whole house to decorate and re-do and then looking at one budget that doesn't allow for all new things. And it's hard for a space to feel comforting and cozy if you know you went into major debt creating it. But there is a way to make the decorating process a little easier on yourself and your wallet, and it's really quite simple: *reduce, reuse, repurpose.*

❧ **REDUCE.** Let's start with reducing the items you already have. Decluttering is the ultimate way to get a fresh start and the number one step in loving your spaces again. I call it the purge, and it always makes me so happy to get rid of the extra stuff I no longer need, whether it's an old table, some antiques I don't want, or home accessories that need replacing. Purging these pieces is a great way to prepare for a new look and might offer a chance to make some money for new items in the space.

❧ **REUSE.** I love reusing items I already have by putting them in a new space or decorating them differently to give them a whole new look and life. The best part? It's free! I get a thrill from taking a cabinet or another piece of furniture, moving it to a new room, and styling it differently. It gives new life to its new location and allows me to refresh both spaces.

❧ **REPURPOSE.** Okay, repurposing might actually be my favorite way to save money on big projects. That lackluster dresser in your guest bedroom? Maybe it's no longer a dresser at all! Maybe it's due for a new life as a dining room buffet or a changing table for the nursery.

With some paint and new hardware, you can completely reinvent pieces and refresh you space. Turn some old post bases into cloche displays, turn an old farm sifter into a planter . . . the possibilities are endless! And these changes don't have to cost a lot.

So instead of staring sadly at your budget, try looking around your home with new eyes. What has worn out its welcome and needs to go? What would look great on a different wall or in a new room? And what can you re-envision as a totally different piece with a new purpose? Close your wallet, get creative, and rediscover what your spaces have to offer.

№10

WREATHS

I truly think that the key to bringing life to a space—other than filling the room with your loved ones—is adding natural elements. Potted plants, garlands, wreaths, and just bringing nature inside in general. All of these things can be investments for things that aren't necessarily custom to your space, so it can seem impossible to find an affordable wreath and garland that fits your style exactly. Here are three tips to make your own DIY wreath for any space:

① Take a strand of garland and bring it together at both ends and attach it with craft wire. Optional: wrap craft wire around the whole garland to make it sturdier.

② Use an embroidery hoop to make a wreath! Take the embroidery hoop and attach florals or greenery around it with hot glue. Optional: attach a doily or a printed garland in the middle of the hoop.

③ Take a garland form found at any craft store and wrap a garland around it and attach it with craft wire. If not a garland, you can use single florals and greenery and attach them individually around the wreath form.

BONUS: Take a simple wreath that you already have or find one and make it your own by inserting your own greens, florals, or other items to make it custom and to fit your décor.

24

A rug can be the anchor of a room or entryway, a staple that brings it all together. It can define both the physical boundaries of a space and its style, all the while making your home a little cozier.

Rug materials can range from natural fiber to wool to synthetic. Everyone has different preferences from style to comfort for their own homes. I personally love a good natural fiber rug like jute because it offers a farmhouse vibe without becoming the focal point. I usually prefer my furniture and other accessories to shine, but don't get me wrong, I love when a rug has a moment as well.

Does a room need a rug? Not necessarily. Sometimes a room without a rug can feel fresh and airy (particularly in the spring and summer!), but if you are wanting to define your space or add a touch of cozy under your feet, think about what a rug can do. Try this: walk through each room of your house and consider where a

new rug might work its magic. Is there a seating area that needs to be "grounded"? An entryway that needs a bit of welcoming warmth? A modern kitchen that could use a softer edge? A boring room that needs a little "oomph"? A bedside that is too cold? The right rug could work wonders!

№ 12

RUG PLACEMENT TIPS

A rug's job, other than being an aesthetically pleasing, durable place for your feet to walk on, is to ground a space. If you choose the wrong size rug, it's not able to do its job. If the rug is too small for the space, it can really just look too weak and not offer any charm. So what size rug do you use? It all depends on what you are working with, but here are a few quick tips to help your rug do its best job:

In the living room, you want all of the furniture in your seating area to be touching the rug. For example, the sofa, chairs, and coffee table should all be at least on the edges of the rug.

In the dining room, you want a rug large enough so that all the table and chairs fit comfortably on the rug with all four legs even when the chairs are pulled back.

Beyond size, a rug needs to fit the space practically and aesthetically as well. When choosing a rug, consider how much traffic the space gets and how it's used. A durable rug is essential for entryways and high-traffic areas. And don't forget to consider the rest of your room and the vibe you are going for. Decide if you need a focal-point rug that pops your color palette or a more neutral rug to bring the space together.

After all those considerations, you can head to the rug store with a tape measure and your confidence. And don't forget to take your shoes off for a "test walk"! Hopefully you'll find the perfect rug that meets your toes' cozy standards.

I love when we all have different opinions. I'm not writing this book because I think I have all the answers. I'm writing because I wanted to share what has worked for us and our home to make it a cozy oasis we love. I'm writing because I've made every mistake in the book and continue to make mistakes, but I hope I can share some of that wisdom I've picked up along the way. I mean, I wouldn't be a good friend if I didn't help you avoid the same mistakes I've made! So what do I mean by "don't wait"? Well, I mean . . . don't wait. Don't wait to make your house a home. Don't wait until you have the perfect piece of furniture or enough money for the perfect flooring or new kitchen cabinets to start creating cozy for you and your family. My motto? Work with what you have in this moment.

When we first moved into our farmhouse three years ago, it was a huge undertaking. It was built in the 1800s but redone in the 1980s. We were eager to rip out all the 80s additions—carpet, wallpaper, and stone walls—that were most definitely not our style. So we had a decision to make. We could either live with the carpet and stone walls and wait until we had enough money to completely redo everything, or we could make some temporary fixes so that we could love our spaces in the meantime. Our decision? *Don't wait.* We ripped up our 30-year-old carpet, painted the subfloor, and put down large rugs for a fix until we decided what to do for permanent flooring. To cover those stone walls, we added faux shiplap over the stones, which was a super affordable fix that not only brightened up the rooms but also made them more our style.

Most recently we were waiting to redo the staircase to our second floor until we had enough money to tile the kick plates the whole way up. Finally, after living with subfloor stairs with staples all over them for months, I was fed up. I once again went

stairs for the rest of our time in this farmhouse.

Isn't that funny? If I had continued waiting for a pricey stair renovation to be in the budget, I wouldn't have known how much I could love those steps with a simple free makeover, and eventually I would have spent a lot more money on something I didn't need.

That's why I truly believe in not waiting for the perfect timing or the perfect item or the perfect budget—because in the meantime you could try a new piece of furniture, a paint color, or another temporary fix that saves you time and money and encourages you to fall in love with the space now rather than later. By experimenting and trying new things, you can hone your style and your craft and escape from any "style box" you have put yourself in. Trying new things in that temporary period can really help you discover the style you love for your home.

the "don't wait" route and decided to go for a temporary fix, thinking that at least we could stop stepping over staples every day and enjoy a more peaceful and beautiful walk to our bedroom. I grabbed some leftover floor paint from another room, painted the stairs, and . . . fell in love. That temporary fix turned into my favorite thing ever, and we wouldn't mind keeping the painted

DWELL

— LIVING ROOM —

A cozy place for loved ones to linger

LIVING ROOM

The living room. It's just one room in the house, but it holds so many great moments—from family get-togethers, to Bible studies, to laughs with friends, to Friday night movies, to sitting and relaxing while decompressing from the day. It's the room where all who enter feel they can put their feet on the coffee table and instantly relax.

I have a sort of top-ten list of amazing living rooms I've had the pleasure of relaxing in over the years. The list starts when I was young and includes my grandparents' gorgeous sunroom, where I would sit and catch them up on all my teen angst. They were always so attentive, so I'd station myself there among the couch pillows and keep talking because it meant so much that they were invested in something that, looking back, must have seemed so silly. On to my later years, the living rooms of my friends became mini havens where I could spill the latest news, celebrate accomplishments, mourn losses, hug, laugh, cry, and just be.

These favorite living rooms didn't leave an impression because they were beautifully decorated, although they all were in their own ways. They were my favorite because of the cozy welcome they each offered. They were real, they were approachable, they beckoned me to come take a seat and stay a while. That's the bliss of a cozy living room—it invites us all to linger, because here you are among friends.

TAKE A SEAT

Creating an inviting seating arrangement in the living room is the number one priority when thinking about creating a cozy space for all your friends and family to congregate. A good furniture layout can make all the difference in the world. In fact, changing the seating arrangement in your living room can instantly take it from cold and sterile to warm and inviting. Of course, living rooms are different sizes and shapes and serve different needs, so I can't address all of them, but here are some quick tips to get you started on creating the coziest space possible in your home.

- **Find the focal point.** Before arranging your living area, come up with a focal point by deciding what the purpose of the room is. Is it to entertain? To enjoy a view of the yard while sipping morning coffee? To watch old movies with the family? All of the above? Maybe you just want to create a seating area to gather together with your loved ones and chat without too many distractions. Knowing the purpose of the living room can help you find its focal point—a television, a fireplace, a beautiful large window—and know which way to face your furniture.

- **If you can't find a focal point, create one!** Hang some beautiful artwork, add a large bookcase, or add a beautiful buffet piece to use as an entertainment center. When you find or create your focal point, arrange your furniture around that, and you should be well on your way to having a cozy living room.

- **Get off the wall.** The number one way you can create an intimate seating arrangement is by getting the furniture off the walls and bringing it in to create a cozy setting

35

where everyone can chat and hang out without straining to hear or see each other. Of course every room is different, but once you determine your focal point, bring that furniture in closer to that focal point to amp the cozy factor up.

Use the rug. Cozy rugs add a soft texture to a room and sometimes bring more color or interest to a space as well, but make your rugs work harder. I love using rugs to anchor and define spaces in a room. They can truly make a living room have the best seating arrangement it can by bringing the space all together. How? Well, the rug is a little cheat sheet to create the perfect seating area. A rug that's too small will make the room even more disjointed, so find one that is large enough so that all the furniture at least touches the rug. It can create instant cohesion!

VINTAGE COLLECTIONS

As a child, I collected many things, including pillows and various little treasures that caught my eye while at garage sales with my mom and dad. I would display many of the trinkets proudly on the shelves in my room. I'm not sure exactly why they were my heart's desire at the time. Maybe I felt grown up to be able to purchase these items with my own quarters, or maybe it was my love for decorating at such an early age. Whatever the reason, nothing made me happier. Collecting is a funny thing, isn't it? We own tons of single items, but then, *Wham*! There's the one thing (or more!) that we can't get enough of. Maybe it reminds us of a favorite place we've traveled or a beloved family tradition. Or maybe we inherited an item that we feel needs companions, each of which will remind us of special people and their heritages.

There's a comfort that comes from a collection, and when it's a vintage collection, there's tons of cozy too. Whether it is indeed a group of items that are a part of your upbringing or simply items that are on top of your treasure-hunt list when you

go picking, a vintage collection reveals a bit of who you are. The items are a great way to tell your story, past or present.

From antique clocks to old wooden crates and everything in between, vintage collections can add so much charm and history to a space: antique panoramic

photos, vintage wooden shoe forms, vintage stamps in a glass display jar, antique flash cards, chippy corbels, antique pottery, and the list goes on. These things are great displayed on their own, but imagine them in a big group—even better! If you are struggling to style shelving in your home, try grouping some vintage finds together, and you will be surprised how quickly they fill up and create a lovely display. There is something about those vintage finds with all their patina that can add an element of cozy that a new store-bought item simply can't.

My collecting started when I was a young child and has certainly evolved over the years, but one thing that has remained is my love for nostalgic collections that help bring a cozy and eclectic style to our home. I still wander garage sales, estate sales, and flea markets for items to display proudly on my shelves. And even today, not much makes me happier.

№ 16

BOOKS

Books are such a staple in a cozy home, whether it's new books set out on a coffee table, favorite bestsellers stacked on a bookshelf ready to grab and read, or cookbooks displayed in the kitchen and waiting for your next yummy creation. They not only add a pretty pop of color, even with just their spines facing out, but they also fill your home with stories, interest, and hominess.

Something about books welcomes guests and makes them feel comfortable. Having people over? A coffee-table book can be a great conversation starter and serve as an informal introduction to the homeowner. At my home, our coffee table offers an ever-changing display of books that reflect what I'm currently passionate about. Right now it's home décor and gardening books, which are fun to talk about when we have visitors.

When you're looking for something with a little more, well, history, antique books are the perfect find. They can make every space instantly pop with a cozy element. Old books can be used to style shelving, to create height in vignettes, to add texture and interest to table displays, and so much more. In fact, I use antique books in every room in our home. If I had to recommend one thing to collect while you are out at flea markets and antique stores, it would be books!

My antique books of choice? Pretty green ones. I have been collecting various shades of vintage green books for some time now, but you could choose any style or color to focus your search. Or don't put boundaries on your hunt, and instead pick up any old book that strikes your fancy or helps to tell the story of the place you call home.

№ 17 WALL TEXTURE

Sometimes no matter what you try, certain rooms still look like a box. If you don't have built-in architecture, the walls can seem rather looming—four giant canvases begging to become something interesting. Drawing the eyes to a large statement piece is a good way to break up all the wall space, but if you overdo it, the room can quickly look cluttered.

We need to get back to basics and rethink the walls themselves! Installing a wall texture or covering might be the perfect option to add contrast and interest to your walls. A wall texture can mean everything from beadboard to stone to brick to wallpaper. So what will work best in your house? For inspiration, I suggest visiting historical homes in the area to see what influenced design in your region many years back. You'll find that historical homes offer tons of classic options that remain stylish today, such as beadboard, board and batten, and (of course) shiplap. For a less timeless look, wallpapers are great for adding pattern to a space. But remember that wallpaper can fall in and out of style based on trends, so just plan on changing it a few years down the road.

If the cost and know-how of installing a wall texture seem overwhelming, there are cheap and easy faux choices that make new walls much more attainable! You don't have to go for an intricate wainscoting if your budget and toolbox are both slim. Look for sheets of faux brick from the hardware store, consider cutting plywood into strips to create faux shiplap, or try a thick textured wallpaper that resembles beadboard. You can even use liquid starch to adhere a roll of fabric to a wall!

Shiplap is clearly one of *my* favorite ways to add a classic wall texture to a space. It provides leading lines of transition and creates a welcoming hominess I love. Maybe that's what makes textured walls so cozy—to me, they represent warmth and craftsmanship. And home. Banish the plain box, and turn a few walls into a lovely backdrop to each day's adventures.

Nº 18

HOW TO HANG SHIPLAP

When it comes to adding texture to a space, shiplap is one of the easiest ways and one that anyone can tackle. We have done a lot of shiplap in our lives. Our first install of shiplap was a cheaper route, ripping a ¼-inch-thick sheet of plywood into 5-inch-wide planks. We used nickels to gap the boards and installed them with a pneumatic staple gun.

The easier, better, and little more expensive way to install is using tongue and groove boards purchased through our local lumberyard. This is the preferred way after doing both, and I will share how to install shiplap referencing that method. Here's what you'll need:

First, using a stud finder, mark out the placement of all your studs. You can use a long level to draw the lines or a chalked snap line. This will take the guesswork out of where to place your nails or staples and ensure the shiplap is fully attached to the wall.

MATERIALS NEEDED:

Stud finder

Level

Pry bar and hammer

Miter saw

Pneumatic nail gun

Nails (2½ inches or longer)

Rubber mallet

Paintable caulk

Caulk gun

Putty knife

Paint

Measure the thickness of the trim and baseboards currently installed in the room. If the trim installed in the room is the same thickness or thicker than the shiplap, you can leave it in place and install around the trim, cutting the boards to meet or butt up against the trim. If the trim is thinner than the shiplap, you will need to remove the trim and baseboards in the room, using a pry bar and hammer.

The next few steps are essentially a wash-and-repeat process to installing ship-lap. Measure the length of the wall, and cut your first board to the right length using the miter saw. Starting from the floor and working your way up, place the first board in place on the wall, and check for level by placing the level across the top of the board and nailing the shiplap board in place with the nail gun. Most of the nail-ing was done on the tongue portion of the tongue and groove boards. I preferred this over nailing on the face throughout the entire installation to save time patch-ing holes later. Once the bottom board is installed, measure and cut the next board. Place the next board on top, and check for level. Keep a scrap piece of the tongue and groove board nearby, in case you need to tap on the board with a rubber mallet to achieve level. This will save any bruising or indentation on the tongue (a dented or bro-ken tongue could cause issues for the next board if the groove isn't able to fit easily in

place). From here, you simply repeat all the way up the wall.

Once complete, re-install your trim and baseboards if needed, fill edges and corners with paintable caulk, and paint away.

GLASS

If someone asked, "What is the coziest texture of them all?" you probably wouldn't say glass. But beautiful glass can finish a room and even be the crown jewel of the space. Picture this: a stack of juice glasses on an open kitchen shelf, gleaming in the light and beckoning guests to grab a no-hassle drink. Now picture a beautiful glass-bead chandelier that glimmers and adds more sparkle to a room than ten diamond necklaces. When you are putting together a vignette and it seems to be missing something, don't forget that glass accent, whether it's a picture frame, cloche, vase, glassware, lamp, or lighting. Glass could be that missing ingredient! You'll be reflecting the light in the room and adding structure without weighing down the arrangement.

TIP: When you use a lot of glass in your decor, cleaning can become a second job. My favorite way to clean clear glass pieces is with a vinegar-water mixture and newspaper. Fill a spray bottle with half white

vinegar and half water. Spray the glass pieces as you would any normal solution, and wipe with newspaper.

CLOCHES

A cloche is a tale as old as time, narrating so many stories. Originally, cloches were created for the garden and placed over less-established plants to protect them from colder weather during the night. Can you imagine a lovelier tool? As much as art is found from the interpretation of nature, design takes that a step further by influencing how we display decor, mimicking how those items were originally used. Today, cloches can still cover and protect plants inside and out, but they can also showcase so many other treasures. Sporting glass finials, these domes add an unexpected texture, give a display a focus and purpose, and become the frosting on the cake of any vignette.

Imagine you have a simple small plant on a table. That's fine as is, but it doesn't make much of a statement. Put a glass cloche over the plant,

and suddenly it gives that plant a purpose, a context. Glass isn't often revered as a warm texture, but when it's a cloche that's paired with the right partner, it tells the perfect cozy story.

TREASURES TO SHOWCASE UNDER CLOCHES

- Books
- Antique clocks
- Little picture frames
- Antique figurine collections like farm animals
- Architectural finds
- Seasonal displays
- Stamp collections
- Natural elements such as feathers
- Candles

ANTIQUE CLOCKS

I have a deep appreciation for the numerous clocks scattered throughout my home and vignettes. My mom works for a large clock manufacturer out of Michigan, and I could remember touring the facility throughout my childhood, seeing the new trending designs, the rich wood textures,

and the modern styles. Needless to say, I found a beauty in how different and unique each clock can be, all while doing the exact same thing—telling time.

Antique clocks add interest to any vignette. Pair them with books, picture frames, or potted plants. Or style several of them in a cohesive group to create a statement piece. To add to your collection, you can spot these guys at antique shops, flea markets, and possibly your local thrift store. They are often priced reasonably, and it's so fun to see each one's uniqueness. And a bonus? Some of them still work!

One of my favorite parts about working in interior design is discovering how styled spaces and décor make me feel. The gentle reminder that comes from my many clocks? *Make time.* Make time to read, to breathe, to call my grandmother. There are many different looks in this bunch of clocks—old and new, big and small—but they are all keepers of time, and I appreciate the reminder to make the best of each moment.

CHIPPY PAINT

I love me some chippy paint—on furniture, decor, barns, even old farmhouses. Chippy paint is the canvas to my creative thoughts. When I see a piece chipping away, revealing the underlying paint colors its previous owners chose, along with gouges worn into the paint that dive well into the wood grain, my imagination takes over, thinking of where that piece has been and how it earned its beautiful character.

Sometimes chippy pieces have weathered actual storms to earn their patina. Corbels are particular favorites; I always think of them exposed to the elements, keeping eye on the city below.

Other times a piece's chips and dents are from a more personal touch. A few years ago, my grandma and grandpa road tripped to North Carolina to visit us. One night during their stay, we all stayed up and played games at the dining-room table. My grandma has tremors in her hands, and after a long night of fun and

laughter, I could clearly see where she had left little gouges and dents in the table from her dominoes and the jewelry she was wearing. So when I see little gashes in furniture, it reminds me of those fun game nights or some other late-night furniture

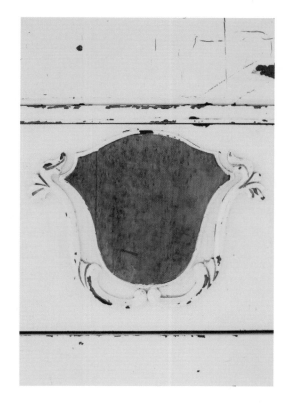

shuffle that resulted in a piece gaining a little beauty mark.

I love our pieces to tell a story, and every dent and scratch on a piece does just that. Some are our stories, and some are stories of someone in the past who loved the piece before us. When we first painted our floors, we had a lot of comments and questions from people wondering why we would do such a thing and what we planned to do if the paint chipped. The answer was simple to us. Painted floors made our home cozier, and we are looking forward to all those dents and scratches because we want our painted floors to tell a story with every chippy board.

Now what to do if you want the chippy paint look in your home, but you can't find that perfect chippy antique? Create the chippy paint look yourself, of course! There are many ways to achieve an antique paint look on a piece, but my favorite is with milk paint. Milk paint comes in a powder form that you mix to your preferred consistency. There is very little prep work if you are wanting a chippy look, and you simply brush it on. After it dries, the magic happens! Milk paint acts differently on every piece because of different variables, but on most it will start to chip off in certain places to give you that naturally worn look. If it doesn't chip as much as you want, you can take a sanding block and manually distress your pieces where it would naturally wear, such as on the edges. After you achieve your desired worn look, simply seal your piece with wax or polyurethane.

When you have new furniture in your home and maybe a few too many uninteresting and unblemished surfaces, mix in some chippy items. Their character will break up the space, add interest and curiosity, and create a cozy room with its own marks of beauty.

TIP: We test everything for lead. You can purchase lead testers and paint-on lead encapsulators at your local hardware store. Don't skip this important step, especially if you have young children. Lead can be very harmful, so make sure your chippy paint is safe for your home.

DIY:

PUT SOME LEGS ON IT

Have you ever noticed that the pieces of furniture you love always have eye-catching legs? Adding legs to a piece of furniture is the simplest DIY in the world, and it's not something everyone thinks of when they pass by a potentially great piece at the flea market. If you are on the fence with a piece because of the lack of height or detail, imagine some legs on that baby and see what you think then!

We've added legs to a bunch of things over the years. The transformation is invaluable. Adding legs to a little entryway table changed its whole tone, and new legs on a sofa table scaled the piece to a practical height.

Sometimes we'll find a table that has a beautiful top but damaged legs or a style of legs that simply does not match the look we are going for. Card catalogs or drawer systems are another great piece to re-envision with a new set of legs. When we

HOW TO ADD LEGS

Most major hardware stores sell furniture legs as well as mounting hardware to make putting legs on anything so simple. All you need is a tape measure and a screwdriver. The legs and mounting hardware are usually found in the lumber section of the hardware store near the dowel section.

The installation is simple: Screw the mounting plates in place on the bottom of your piece. The purchased legs come with pre-installed hanger bolts, so you can screw those directly onto the attached mounting plates.

purchased this card catalog, it had hairpin legs that seemed out of place since most pieces in our home have chunkier legs. So we swapped them out, which also lowered the piece to better fit behind the sofa.

Now where can you find some new legs? You can try your local hardware store or craft store and online suppliers, or you could even get creative and DIY your own

with a 4x4, trim or molding, and a router. Or if you have a wood lathe, you could spin a set yourself. For this example, let's stick with buying legs. We found some at our local hardware store and added them to this somewhat non-functional set of drawers that sat low to the ground.

To make the drawer set work in our sunroom, it needed to be higher, so we simply added the legs to the bottom. We painted the legs the same color as the rest of the piece, and that was it. The result was a set of drawers that was the right height for the space and functioned like a table—a one-of-a-kind table that now stands out since it has a great set of legs to stand on.

№ 25

PUT SOME WHEELS ON IT

If you aren't thinking legs are the best upgrade to your piece of furniture, what about wheels? I love adding legs to just about any piece of furniture that doesn't have any, but sometimes wheels do it more justice. If you need a piece just lifted up a few inches or if you want to make something more mobile, it's easy to add wheels. Try it on the bottom of a dresser or any piece of furniture. Just like adding furniture legs, you can find new wheels at your local hardware store, or really cool ornate antique ones can be uncovered at flea markets and vintage shops.

N⁰ 26 FIREPLACE FOCAL POINT

We all have different visions of what cozy is, but I would bet that a majority of us instantly feel cozier when a fireplace is in the room. We picture ourselves snuggling up close, listening to the flames popping, and feeling the softness of our favorite cotton blanket against our feet. Add a good book in our hands and a hot cocoa by our side, and we've got ourselves a universal call to get cozy.

The fireplace also gets extra points for offering premiere real estate for display: the mantel. Let's make that area showcase items that define your style, the room, your family, or your current mood. There's no pressure—you can change your mantel design as often as you want! But always make it something you want people to notice when they enter the room. Here are some ideas of what to showcase:

- A framed map
- A framed piece of cloth
- A grouping of plates
- A large-scale clock
- A favorite piece of your child's artwork
- A flat basket
- An antique mirror, particularly an oxidized one
- A quirky, unexpected piece such as your grandfather's guitar or a vintage sign
- Salvaged architectural pieces (my favorite, of course, is something chippy!)

Once you've chosen the focal point that's right for your mantel, here are a few other ways to make sure your fireplace is inviting, no matter the season:

Position your furniture to face the fireplace, and then pull it all in closer together than you think you should. Seriously. Too many people end up with super-spacious conversation groupings that make it hard to enjoy both the conversation and the warmth of the fire. As long as your main seating is at least three feet from the flames, you're good.

Make sure there's a hearth or low table near the fireplace where books and coffee mugs can happily land.

If you don't have a hearth, consider adding low seating such as a simple bench or ottoman that can easily (and safely) be pulled close to the flames on chilly nights.

Don't be afraid to paint any stone, brick, or wood that surrounds the fireplace. Just do your research to make sure you're using the right products for the material and the heat level. Even a slight change in paint color can make a huge difference.

In the off-season when you aren't building fires, add a houseplant to the mantel or hearth so that something green and living can help balance the "black hole" of the firebox.

Have fun finding and showcasing your own favorite fireplace focal point. Then be sure to invite those you love to share one of the most inviting spaces in your home!

№ 27

COMFY THROWS

Sofas are pretty cozy on their own; well, most are. Picture your home's sofa, or an armchair or bed. Now picture it with a comfy throw blanket draped across it. Imagine an oversized, textured throw with gorgeous nubby weave. So much cozier, huh?

A chunky throw can make a world of difference when trying to warm up a room, and you probably don't have to spend money or time to do it (unless you want a new throw!). We most likely all have one stored in a drawer or closet that we can pull out to drape over a seat, calling someone to gather and sit in the space. A soft, luxurious throw can make a cold piece of furniture—and a home—feel instantly warm and inviting.

Try draping a throw blanket over the back of a couch, on the seat of a reading chair, over the entire bed, or just at the end. Which option looks most welcoming? Throws can be displayed in a million ways, and honestly it can be quite an art form

(maybe we should add "throw-draping" as a new category of art!).

How to naturally drape a throw or blanket is one of the most frequent questions I get on the blog, and it is one of the hardest techniques to explain. Let me start with the end result and work my way backward. When you walk into a room and see an effortlessly draped throw lying across the front edge of a cozy sofa or across the arm of your favorite chair, it's much like the welcoming feeling you get as a friendly face greets you. When you stage the throw perfectly, you'll see a seating area that is fresh and crisp, waiting for you to kick up and relax.

The art is making it look as effortless as possible. Grab the literal center of the throw or blanket. Take the bunched-up fabric that is in your hand and place that toward the back of the sofa allowing the open end to drape across the front edge of the sofa or arm of the chair. It should be a toss and slight fluff of the edges. Again, the goal is natural and effortless.

Play stylist and practice more ways to display cozy throws:

- Stacked in an open-door cabinet or on the seat of a seldom-used occasional chair
- Rolled in a basket next to the sofa, ready to grab
- Folded neatly over the back of the sofa or at the end of a bed
- Draped over the edge of an open trunk

Here's a little irony for you: once you perfect your rolling/folding/draping technique with your favorite throws, don't think twice about unrolling, unfolding, and undraping them when it's time to enjoy the cozy spot you've created! At least once a week, commit to taking some time for yourself to grab your blanket and curl up with a cup of tea and your favorite book, magazine, or movie. Allow yourself, and your throw blankets, to relax. You can always return them to their folded glory to await your next break. After all, cozy is only cozy if we actually live it and enjoy it.

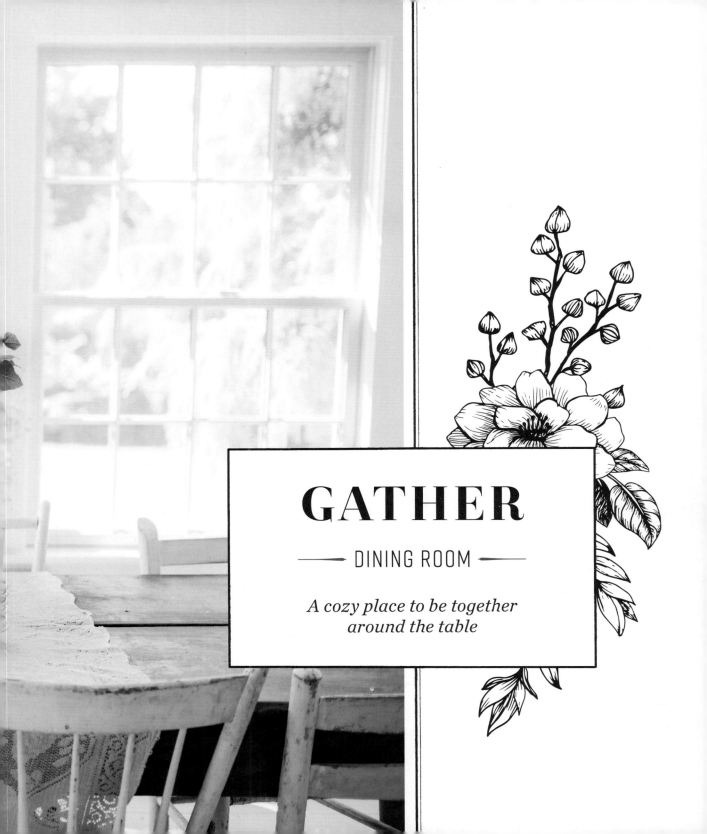

GATHER

— DINING ROOM —

*A cozy place to be together
around the table*

DINING ROOM

In a cozy home, the dining room is a place to linger . . . sharing stories, celebrating milestones, and taking just one more bite. Here the humble table becomes the master of ceremonies, turning us toward each other and centering our attention on the blessings of food, friends, and family.

It's a place where our sense of cozy comes not only from our full bellies but also from our full spirits. They seem to know that a chair at the table means a place to belong. This room is where we gather—to know our people a little better, to break bread, to build traditions that outlast the years. Fill your dining room with beautiful things and beautiful hearts, and it will reward you with its bounty.

№ 28 WHITE STONEWARE

Timeless white stoneware is one of my absolute favorite things to collect. Stacked on shelves, it makes a cozy statement while adding tons of texture to a dining room or kitchen. Plus, it's practical. Use stoneware plates as your daily dishes, fill a stoneware pitcher with flowers, or use a small stoneware platter to corral keys and pocket change.

Want a different way to display your stoneware? Hang plates and platters on the walls to add some unique antique art to any room in your home. They also make great additions to gallery walls, nestled among family photos or framed art. Your local craft or hardware store should stock hangers that make it super simple to hang any size plate or platter on the wall.

No matter what changes in my style, stoneware will always be a classic item my husband and I actually use in our daily life. It reminds me that our homes are not meant to be photo sets. They are meant to be lived in. So when we surround ourselves with cozy spaces and décor that are lovely to look at *and* lovely to use, life becomes a little more pretty while also moving a little more smoothly. That's the key.

I have a vintage stoneware platter that is the perfect size for serving my home-baked bread. Every time I fill it with fresh slices, I think of the stories it could tell of the women before me who filled the same platter with home-baked goodness. It makes me value this simple piece of stoneware all the more, and that's practical loveliness at its best.

No 29
SHELF STYLING 101

I'm often asked, "How do you style a shelf?" Well, my answer is usually, I just go with it. I play around until I like it, and then I quit. But I realize that answer is not particularly helpful to my friends who have "shelf anxiety."

My shelf-anxious friends too often grab some random items, line them up, and end up unhappy with the results because it looks much like a shelf at their local big box store. My goal is always to have things look collected but not decorated.

So before you start, go and grab your favorite collections, whether those are books, bottles, clocks, vintage pottery, or whatever collected items make you smile. Okay, are you back now? The key is not to go out and buy all new things for your shelves. This is the perfect chance to show off the things you love! Of course, after looking through your collections, you can see what items you need to fill in the blanks later and then purchase a few.

Let's get started and decorate those shelves in four easy steps:

1. **Start from the bottom.** I don't always do this because I'm kind of scattered when I decorate. That said, it's important to put the heaviest items—whether those are physically heavy or visually heavy because they are large—on the bottom so the shelves feel grounded, balanced, and not top-heavy.

2. **Make it useful.** Make it useful for your family, whether that's adding storage in your shelves with cute baskets or displaying a child's artwork or something special to your family. Let the shelves tell your family's story without being too stuffy or looking too decorated.

3. **Have fun arranging!** Keep the items cohesive, such as mercury glass and different natural textures that all work together nicely to create balance on

the shelves. If you're using books, try placing them different ways, like horizontally stacked or with the spines facing the wall. Don't be afraid to set art on the shelves to balance out pieces of a similar size. If I can recommend anything else, it's to add a little greenery! In my opinion, plants, whether real or faux, are the secret sauce that make shelves pop.

4. **Keep playing with it.** Step back and take a look at your work. A little trick I usually do is photographing the shelves. That will often show the flaws in your work. A photo isn't as forgiving as the naked eye. Take a look at the photo and see if some of your balance is off or if there are empty spots you need to fill.

Nº 30

WICKER

I'm not talking about your grandma's wicker chair. Or maybe I am? It's all in how you style it, and to me wicker is an excellent way to bring texture into a room. Bring in wicker chairs, baskets, placemats, or other accents to any space that seems a bit bland, and choose brown wicker pieces when you need to add warmth to an all-white space.

You can find classically styled wicker pieces at your favorite home décor store, but unique vintage pieces can be thrifted or found at your local antique shops. My opinion? Wicker looks best a little worn! More texture, more character, more stories they can tell. Wicker chairs are great outside on a porch or patio, but gathering wicker chairs around a dining-room table can truly bring the outdoors in and give your space a cozy cottage greenhouse vibe.

N° 31

BASKETS FILLED WITH STEMS

Baskets are an amazing way to add texture to a space, but do you know what happens when you put some beautiful seasonal stems *into* the basket? Pure magic. One day I was walking around our home, and all of the sudden I realized every room had some kind of basket with stems in it. Every single room! I never noticed it was something I did, but I guess it's a natural thing for me to plop some stems into a basket to bring life into a room. The best part? It's so simple and only takes the effort to find the basket and the stems. Every home décor store offers various basket styles, but this is also another item to find at your local antique or thrift shop. The more unique the better.

I have a collection of wicker baskets I've collected over the years, and I love to keep them handy for styling. For the stems, I've used everything from greens to cotton to a whole potted plant. The possibilities are endless! You can use a basket of stems as an impressive table centerpiece, hang the basket on a door, or even put it on the floor. Hey, that rhymed! Well, it makes sense because a basket with stems in it is pure poetry.

Nº 32

FAUX GREENERY

We all wish we had the best green thumb in the world. Wouldn't it be great to be able to keep a plant longer than a week and to have a home filled with fresh greens at all times? Well, sometimes, it just doesn't work. I have started to really develop my green thumb since moving to the farm, and I'm really proud of that. I've even joined a garden club this year! Yes, much of it involves us girls chatting about life, but we do talk plants too, and I think I've now become a crazy plant lady. However, many places *inside* our home aren't ideal for real plants, and that is where faux greenery comes in.

Faux greens can be tricky because sometimes they take the "faux" too far. To find options that look real, I have two suggestions. First, do a tiny bit of research before you shop. Look up the actual plant that the faux plant is impersonating to see how closely it resembles the real thing. If it's an olive tree, does it *look* like the coloring of a real olive tree? Are the leaves too shiny? Too matte? Second, when you're in the store, I highly suggest touching the leaves. Do they *feel* real? The ones that do most likely look real too, and that's what you want. I love finding some of my favorite faux greens at Pottery Barn, Amazon, Pier 1, Michaels, and many other places.

When you choose the right faux greenery, it's surprising how much life it can bring to any space, bringing a touch of the outdoors to dining and living rooms and on into the office and laundry room. Consider greenery to be the icing on the vignette. If you can't go real, go faux!

N° 33

VINTAGE LIGHT FIXTURES

So many interesting new lighting options are available these days, but there will always be something about the patina of vintage light fixtures. Authentic vintage lights are unique works of art! Modern fixtures may try to replicate those antique one-of-a-kind design elements, but often those don't use the same vintage materials. So be on the lookout at flea markets or dig through some salvage for table lamps, ceiling fixtures, or floor lamps with unique details you can't find anywhere else.

If you discover a vintage light fixture that stops you in your tracks, how can you incorporate it into your home? Consider a couple tips.

⚜ **CONSULT WITH THE SELLER.** Ask whether a fixture has been rewired to meet today's safety standards. If any of the wires are brittle or frayed, it could be a fire hazard. The seller may also be able to recommend a bulb type or wattage appropriate for the specific piece.

⚜ **CONSULT WITH A LICENSED ELECTRICIAN.** Some pieces are so affordable that they are worth taking to a licensed electrician. An electrician or lighting store can rewire fixtures for you and help with installation.

Oh, the classic and oh-so-coveted window seat. What is it that makes window seats so magical? They scream, "Please come cuddle up on me with a good book and some tea!" Because of my love for cozy little nooks, I have always dreamed of having a window seat. This year we finally made that come true, and it was as easy as building a mobile bench and setting it in front of a window in our breakfast nook. It's built to fit the little space squeezed between the cabinets in the kitchen and the windows in our sunroom; so it looks built in, like it came with our 1800s farmhouse. We even added some drawers to our window seat for extra storage, which is an amazing perk in an old house. To add softness, we used two bench cushions side by side. Dreams can come true, friends!

You too might be able to create a cozy little window seat in your home! Do you have a window at the end of a hall? Or between two bookcases in the bedroom?

What about a breakfast corner that needs more seating? Remember, you don't have to have an old home to create a nook. With a little cozy thinking and not much money, you might be able to squeeze in a magical window seat of your very own. For full DIY instructions, check out LizMarieBlog.com/cozywhitecottagebook.

№ 35

CANDLES

I once asked my Facebook community what they thought made a home cozy, and the number one answer was "smell/candles." I was shocked! I thought for sure it would be "a big cozy couch" or "cozy pillows and throws." Nope, it was scent. It makes total sense, so I don't know why I was so shocked, but that got me thinking. What smells do people find cozy? So I did a survey, and the answers ranged widely—from light and airy cucumber melon to warm and savory pumpkin pie.

As for me, I tend to pick either fresh masculine scents that smell clean with sandalwood undertones or kitchen scents like rosemary mint.

We might all prefer different candle scents, but let's agree that they are simply cozy and we should burn them more often. Perhaps a part of their cozy factor is that they evoke certain feelings and bring back memories. My sense of smell has always

been strong, and my mom says that scents were very important to me even when I was young. Particular smells have always brought back memories and probably make up the strongest part of my memory bank. I'll walk into a store, and a certain smell will take me back to my grandma's home when I was growing up, or I'll walk through

a crowd and smell my grandpa's after-shave. Sigh.

So many great warm-and-fuzzy feelings can come from scent, so no wonder it has the power to completely change how a room feels. When it comes to adding delicious scent to your home, candles are the simplest answer yet make a dramatic difference. A single candle in a vignette with its flickering, fiery wick can add just the right glow to any room and give your home just the right amount of cozy too.

I have to say that after years of burning many candles, I have become a candle snob—not all candles are made the same! I'm a fan of clean-burning soy candles that use essential oils and have good wicks. A quality candle that has a long burn time and doesn't lose its scent is the perfect splurge, a little slice of sensory luxury that we, and our memories, deserve.

N° 36 DECORATING WITH CANDLES

I don't do many tablescapes that don't involve candles. Why? Because they are the international sign of "Please come gather at the table and dine with me." Don't fact check me on that, but a set of candlesticks in the center of a table makes everyone who gathers there feel cozy and open to good conversation and good food. One or two candlesticks mixed in with a centerpiece is all you need, but a big group of them in the middle of the table can make a glowing statement and fill a centerpiece quickly.

CENTERPIECE TIP: For the simplest and quickest centerpiece, lay a bed of greenery (either faux or real) down the entire useable center of the table. Top with candlesticks.

CANDLE TIP: It doesn't have to be a real candle to feel warm and cozy. There are some great faux, battery-powered candles that look quite realistic and can give the same effect. The best part is there is no worry about leaving them on, and they'll keep "burning" until the last dinner guest says goodnight.

№ 37
WINDOW TREATMENTS

One way to anchor any room of your home and instantly add a cozy factor is with window treatments. They're the icing on the cake after you have picked your cozy paint color, added a rug, added furniture, and decorated your space. After doing all that, you may still feel like something is missing. If you need more texture or privacy, window treatments are that missing factor that can make you feel safer and warmer as you snuggle in to your spaces.

Window treatments—from roman shades to curtain panels to blinds of all colors and textures—are one of my favorite ways to ground a space and make it feel complete. Done the right way, window treatments can make a room feel high end and cozy, and that's a win-win in my book!

My biggest suggestion is to hang your curtains high and wide. I like to hang them at least six inches above the window if possible. Hanging curtains high draws your eye up, making the ceiling look higher, the window larger, and the room bigger. Also, don't be afraid to hang your curtains wider than the window, up to ten inches and beyond! Your window treatments will make a bigger statement this way.

When you're deciding on window treatments, consider the mood you want to create. The style and even length of curtains can add a different feel to a room. For a casual look, choose lengths that pool slightly on the floor. For a more tailored look, choose panels that just skim the floor. If you want to add some romance or drama to your space, choose extra-long lengths that can create big puddles on the floor. What could be cozier?

№ 38 LEADED GLASS WINDOWS

I've had a liking for stained-glass and leaded-glass windows since I was a child. I know it's because they seem to tell so many stories. I love to imagine the buildings they once were on, the things people saw as they looked out of them, and what went on beyond them within the homes they adorned.

My grandpa worked on stained glass as a hobby and still does to this day. He used colored glass to make beautiful art pieces, from lamps to window art. As a child, I marveled at the way the pieces turned out, and I appreciated them more because I was able to see the hard work that went into making each and every one. I remember watching his hands cut out the glass shapes and fit them together like a puzzle, sometimes not knowing what he was creating. He would finally hold up the finished piece to reveal that it was a flower all along. I still have a stained-glass lamp that Grandpa created

for me when I was little, and I can't wait to add it when I finish Cope's nursery.

When we first saw the farmhouse (before it was ours), we were thrilled it had leaded-glass windows in some of the rooms. They add stunning charm to the house, and they are one of the reasons I fell in love with it instantly. But I also love finding and bringing home leaded-glass windows from antique stores and flea markets. These discovered pieces are great to hang on a wall, set in a vignette, and even hang over an already existing window (a great trick if your home has plain, builder-grade windows). The best part? Leaded-glass windows are even more gorgeous when the light is shining through them. Next time you are at an antique shop or a flea market, see if you can spot one! If you bring it home, don't be surprised if you find yourself wondering about the scenes it might have framed long ago.

ANTIQUE SIGNS

I have this obsession with antique signs. As I'm walking the rows of flea markets, nothing stops me in my tracks faster than an antique sign that is advertising "Honey for Sale" or "Vegetables Next Left." Chippy old signs like these can be found all over flea markets and antique stores with different color combinations of words and styles.

The big box stores are full of some lovely modern-day signs with hand-lettered quotes and bits of inspiration. But years ago, a hand-lettered sign had a much more practical use! I can't help but be drawn to these black-and-white antiques that used to be on the side of the road selling farm goods. Today, they can become the focal point of a room and be that conversation piece you've been looking for. Whether it's a farm sign or a colorful vintage sign that once sold soda pop at a gas station, these advertisements make for some fruit-of-the-earth coziness when brought home and hung on your walls! And if you ever decide to sell your own honey by the roadside, you'll be all set.

N° 40

BACKGROUND MUSIC

My goal for our home is to make it cozy for our family, but I often make small adjustments when we have company over to make them feel cozy in our home when they visit. What started as a habit when visitors come over has turned into a daily ritual that literally makes our home sing with happiness. That ritual? Music. It's that simple flip of a switch to turn on our family's favorite playlist that instantly boosts our moods and inspires family dance parties in the dining room.

We love playing music when guests are over to help them feel more welcome in our home. Music can also be a great way to help people feel more relaxed and at home, and sometimes it can be a great ice breaker as well! When we welcomed our first child into our home, I did a little research on why we play lullabies for babies. The articles I found explained that music stimulates neurons in babies' brains that turn fear or sadness into relaxation.

Guess what? It doesn't stop when we grow up either. Different types of music stimulate different neurons in our brain. Depending on the mood you want to create, choose your music accordingly.

TIP: We love using wireless Bluetooth speakers that connect right to our phones' playlists so the speaker can be heard yet hidden, with no wires to decorate around.

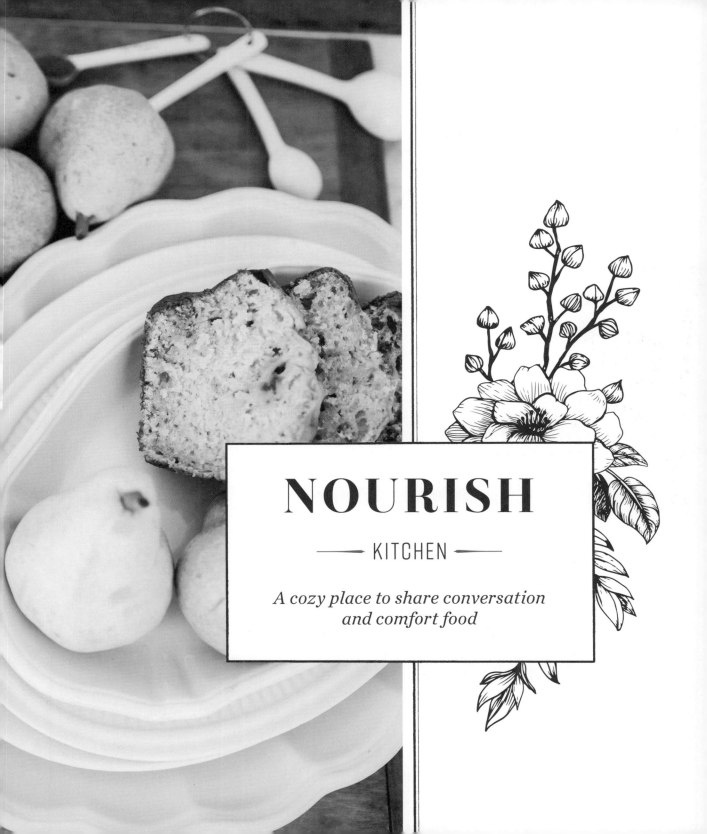

NOURISH

— KITCHEN —

*A cozy place to share conversation
and comfort food*

KITCHEN

Often called the heart of the home, the kitchen is where many of our strongest memories are forged—memories of being greeted with a favorite after-school snack and learning to make Grandma's unforgettable spaghetti sauce. It's a room made for emotional ties.

The kitchen is where we nourish our families, but we nourish them with much more than just food. Here we fill others with comfort, belonging, warmth, and sustenance. Sometimes the nourishment is in the form of hot soup or cold tea, but often it's an early-morning hug while still in pajamas or the camaraderie of a late-night snack.

Standing around the kitchen island, or playing cards around the table, we find ourselves building memories here that nourish our souls. Welcome to the heart of cozy. Come fill your plate.

No 41

KITCHEN SHELVES

Open shelving can be just as much of a statement in the kitchen as a farmhouse sink or a one-of-a-kind kitchen island. It also forces you to keep a clean and simple collection of plates, bowls, and

cups, because your dishware is always on display. Although the items on the shelves are usually the center of attention, you can balance the space below and between the shelves by incorporating unique items such as vintage corbels or architectural pieces. Antique corbels used as brackets for shelving do more than just provide support. They also add a level of texture and ensure that your shelves are never boring.

I have friends who wonder how I keep my open shelves clean and dust free, and here's my answer: it's easier than you think! For my dishware shelves, these are the pieces that we use every day, so they're being moved and removed over and over. And you know me, I'm always trying a different arrangement when I return them to the shelf. You'll find there's not much time for dust to even settle in! When I'm unloading the dishwasher and restocking the shelf, I sometimes make a swipe with the dish towel too. That's about all it takes!

Having white dishes also helps keep the look neat; they offer a clean and streamlined look even when on full display. And I might suggest you think twice about too many small or unnecessary items in this utilitarian area. This is for your hardworking pieces! So limit your collection, use every cup and bowl and plate with love, and let them work hard for you while on full display.

CLEANING CHART

Doesn't a clean home feel cozier? When the days and the weeks get busy, a cleaning schedule that fits your lifestyle and that is obtainable for you and your family will help you keep the house tidy and clean. The schedule could be simply mentally recording what you need to do each day and making a habit of it. Or you could make a printable chore chart for the whole family so that you all get into a rhythm of what needs to be done and can keep each other and your home in check. For a little help, I have a printable cleaning chart on my blog at lizmarieblog.com.

TEA TOWELS

The simple tea towel. We collect them, use them, and gift them. But did you know they can make some pretty amazing decor? A simple tea towel can be placed on the edge of the sink, draped on the counter by a cutting board, hung on a hook, used as a table linen under a centerpiece, or basically dropped anywhere. The linen texture instantly makes a cold kitchen look more inviting and lived in.

Want another great use for tea towels? Make some art! That's right . . . have you ever admired the cute designs on tea towels? We have been using a trick for years that works every single time: we make a DIY frame out of reclaimed wood pieces and fit it around the towel. Once it's fastened on to a piece of plywood, *voilà*! . . . instant beautiful art with warmth and texture! The best part is that the art is custom and unique to you and your home.

HARDWARE

Although it's small, hardware is a critical element when bringing your home from average to upscale. You might think I'm only referring to the knobs and pulls in the kitchen and bath. But if you stop and look around your space right now, you'll be surprised at just how many items have hardware on them . . . from dressers to doors, coat hooks to cabinets. Maybe you bought some new pieces or moved into a new home and haven't yet considered replacing the hardware. Let's do it!

Changing out the hardware is a simple project that can make a huge immediate difference in a space. You can find hardware options at antique shops, flea markets, and craft stores as well as kitchen shops and specialty stores. Choosing custom hardware that reflects your personal style can make your home so unique and give it the finished look you've been craving. Let's think of the hardware as the jewelry of your space—don't forget the jewelry!

№ 45

WALL SCONCES

This is a big one. This isn't your grandma's art gallery wall sconce that resembles a piano light. Nope, this is a wall sconce that gives light to an otherwise dark location, that adds interest and a focal point to a seemingly boring part of your wall, and that just makes a space seem finished.

I know what you may be thinking: *I can't have a wall sconce because I don't have an electrical box on my walls.* I've got you covered. For some sconces in our home, we didn't want to remove all the pre-installed electrical stuff within the light, in case we wanted to hardwire them somewhere later on. So to preserve the lights, we simply placed puck lights inside them! You can buy puck lights with remotes from online retailers like Amazon. Batteries are built into each puck light, and it does not have long wires or a separate battery compartment that would require stringing it through to the base of the light.

HOW TO INSTALL WALL SCONCES WITHOUT WIRING

To install, put a fresh set of batteries in the puck light. Turn the shade of the sconce up so it is facing the ceiling. Using removable Velcro adhesive strips (such as Command Strips), stick the puck lights inside the shades where the light bulb would go. Another option is to apply a consistent and generous layer of silicone adhesive around the perimeter of the puck light and follow the curing instructions on the adhesive packaging. Once the silicone has cured, it will have a similar consistency to caulk. If you apply a generous layer, it usually will come off in one piece if you later need to remove the puck light. But for now, you're ready to hang your sconces and light a little corner of your world!

COFFEE BAR

If you don't know by now, I have a deep relationship with coffee. I grew up drinking coffee (mainly decaf) with my grandpa, and we would dip windmill cookies in it. When I was sixteen, my first job was a barista at a local coffee shop. At one point I was a barista at two coffee shops at once. I loved the job, and most of all, I loved the coffee! Having a cup of coffee in my hand is comforting to me; it's like my security blanket.

If you are a coffee drinker, or if you have guests who are, set aside a little corner of your kitchen for a coffee station or coffee bar. I don't function without coffee, so keeping the essentials out for easy access means I can make my next cup in a snap. It also helps company feel welcome because they can help themselves.

To set up your coffee station, of course you'll need to start with your coffee maker of choice, whether it's a pour over, French press, or basic brewer. Add a mug rack and your favorite coffee mugs. Then style your coffee and condiments, like sugar, cinnamon, or flavored syrups, in canisters to keep everything organized. When you have visitors, make bottled water and tea available as well so they feel right at home.

N<u>o</u> 47

STOVE TOP POTPOURRI

There's nothing cozier or more inviting than the smell of something yummy simmering on the stove top. If you've never tried stove top potpourri, you need to! The beauty of it is that you can use items you already have on hand, and there's no specific recipe to follow. Start with your favorite fruits, spices, and fresh herbs. Here are a few combinations to try:

- Orange slices (or even just the peel), rosemary sprigs, whole vanilla bean, and a bay leaf
- Lemon slices (or just the peel), mint leaves, rosemary sprigs, and a whole vanilla bean
- Apple slices, orange slices (or just the peel), peeled ginger root, cinnamon sticks, cloves, and cardamom

Place your items in a pot or Dutch oven, cover it with water, bring it to a boil, and then reduce the temperature to low to simmer. That's it! As the potpourri cooks down, you can add more water. You can even refrigerate it, add more water, and reheat it.

If you want to fill every corner of your home with warmth and coziness using only natural ingredients, create your own DIY stove top potpourri!

DIY:

TOPIARY

Topiaries are a lovely way to add some structured greenery to your space. And if you don't have a green thumb or lack a positive track record for keeping plants alive for longer than a week, don't worry. We can DIY some faux topiaries! Here is what you'll need.

MATERIALS NEEDED:

Hot glue gun

Glue sticks

Sheet of moss

Tree branch

Boxwood garland

Terracotta flower pot

Spray foam

Nail clippers

① First, place the small tree branch in the center of the flower pot. Spray foam the stick in place, filling the pot about half full. When the foam expands, you want it to be as close

to flush across the top of the pot as possible. If the foam expands above the top of the pot, use a piece of fishing line to cut the foam flush across the top.

② Next, install the sheet of moss on top of the foam across the top of the pot. Most sheet moss purchased at a craft store has a sticky side. If not, use the hot glue gun to attach it to the foam.

③ Pull apart the boxwood garland and hot glue the pieces to the tree branch in an organic fashion to look like a real topiary. Repeat this step until you have a full topiary. Use the nail clippers to clip away any excess dried hot glue strings or globs.

Nº 49

STAY IN YOUR SEASON

If you get any tip from this book I hope it's this: We are all in different seasons of life, we are all walking different paths, we all live with different purposes, and we all should focus on making each season of our lives beautiful. When we do, we can move into the next season with grace, look back, and be proud.

So what does this have to do with making our homes cozy? A lot. When we go on social media or visit someone else's home, we naturally compare and start to log in our minds what our homes are lacking in comparison. Don't get me wrong—it's always great to get inspired and make a dream checklist for our homes, but there is a line we can so easily cross . . . where we look up from a beautiful interior shot on our phones and begin to hate our house and only see what's wrong with it.

But let's really think about the season of life you are in. . . . Maybe you are taking care of a newborn, chasing toddlers, saving up for your dream home, living the military life, taking on a fixer-upper, working hard on your career, waiting to start a family, or somewhere in between all of that. All our lives are so different, so how can we logically compare what we have to someone else in that exact time? We can't, but that doesn't mean we don't do it. Can I challenge you to stop doing that? To look around your home and see the good in it? To stop comparing your home's season to someone else's? Can I challenge you to stay in your season of life and hunker down and enjoy the good in it? Use the tools, items, and knowledge you have in *this* season to make your home the coziest for you and your family. Don't go into debt trying to make your home like someone else's, don't make your family uncomfortable trying to mimic how someone else's house functions when your family isn't the same, and don't let comparison ruin your view of your cozy home.

Enjoy this season of life. Soon it will be gone, and whether the season is hard or easy street, it comes with important parts that teach us things we will one day miss. So stay in your season, and embrace it.

ADDING THE FIVE SENSES

To turn up the cozy, quickly add the five senses to any space.

1. **Smell:** Light a candle or bake something yummy to get your house smelling cozy. Or bring home some fresh flowers.

2. **Sight:** Do a five-minute pickup of the space, and use this time to declutter, to freshen things up, and to make the room look more relaxed.

3. **Touch:** Add a comfy throw or pillow

to any space to give it that instant cozy vibe. Have a little more time? Add a rug to define the space and amp up the cozy factor.

4. **Hearing:** Take a minute to pamper your ears and your mind with something that is cozy and soothing, whether it's music, a podcast, background noise, or silence. You might try a cozy-inspired playlist too. We created one on Spotify called "Cozy White Cottage" that we'd love to share with you.

5. **Taste:** Grab a cup of coffee or tea to curl up in your cozy spot. I like to have my current favorite drink waiting so I have a little luxury to look forward to when I settle down in the evening. As I write this, I'm sipping on sweet tea. Allowing yourself to taste that little luxury gives all the cozy vibes from the outside in.

N⁰ 51 LETTING LOOSE

You know those really awkward moments you get into at parties where you feel like you have to pretend to be someone else and you can't find one thing to talk about because you just can't relax and be yourself? Maybe I'm more awkward than your average person, or maybe I'm more introverted than I know, but this has happened to me way too often.

Finally, after years of not knowing how to classify or control these feelings, I slowly came to realize that my own discomfort was causing others to be uncomfortable around me. A while back I asked a few close friends what their definition of *cozy* was, and one of them said, "Wherever I feel like I can let loose and just be myself." Right then and there the answer came to me. To create a comfortable home, we must feel comfortable with ourselves, and to make others cozy, we must feel cozy with ourselves.

Imagine having a friend over and sharing a relaxed afternoon and a pot of coffee. You are truly able to be in the moment and be fully invested in the conversation because you're not busy apologizing for the state of your house or worrying about what she thinks. You're comfortable, and you've created an environment where others aren't afraid to be themselves and can use your home like it's their own. You can let loose, and so can they. . . . Everyone can be feet-up-on-the-coffee-table comfy. No matter what your home looks like at the moment, claim it as your own. Remember, if it's cozy to you, it's cozy to others too.

RENEW

— BATHROOM —

A cozy place to pamper

BATHROOM

When we think of a bathroom, we don't always think *cozy*. But as the self-proclaimed queen of all things cozy, I can tell you that the bathroom can actually be one of the coziest spots in the house. Why? Well, water has an innate ability to restore and *renew*, so the bath is where we can clean off the day (both mentally and physically).

As soon as you shut the door and step into a hot bath or a steamy shower, you can escape from reality with some yummy smelling lavender, cozy towels, and a clean and organized space. Turning your bathroom into a tiny oasis can be a simple project, whether your bathroom is a room that can fit twenty people or as tiny as a hall closet. Like most other ways to make your home cozy, it doesn't have to be complicated, but it can totally change how you are able to relax and renew in your bathroom.

N<u>o</u> 52 SOAPS, SCENTS, AND MEMORIES

My grandma used to collect the most beautiful soaps in a big bowl in her bathroom. I just figured that's what every grandma had in her home. I would look at the beautiful wrapping around each soap and smell it through the paper. I'm sure the little designer in me tried to rearrange the soaps in some fashion too.

I remember walking into the bathroom at her home and instantly feeling pampered and wrapped up in warmth. The room wasn't large, but it was grand in its own way . . . from the smell of the French soaps in the bowl to the cold tile and plush rugs against my toes, from the clean, crisp towels for the guests to the beams of sun coming through the window. Looking back, I'm sure my grandma put a ton of effort into making each room of her home welcoming, even her bathrooms. I can still remember how one smelled like her fancy soaps and the other smelled like my grandpa's aftershave, but both left impressions on me.

I would say your home is welcoming and cozy if someone can talk about your bathroom being a place of luxury and warmth even if it's the smallest space in your home and the last place we think to make cozy. Your bathroom can make an impression on your day and on your guests, so why not make it cozy? Ever since those young years, I've been drawn to nice soaps and try to keep them in our baths, even in our fixer-upper. Our guests might be walking on exposed subfloor, but they will have yummy soaps to use, which I hope makes up for it all.

When we first got married, Jose was in the military and we lived far from home. This meant we had many visitors. I was always trying to find ways to make our guests more comfortable when they came to visit us. One thing I have always done is collect samples. You know, the shampoo samples, lotion samples, perfume samples, and more. I stored my sample collection in a large glass jar in the guest bathroom so that guests could pick through the samples to find anything that they needed during their stay. It always makes guests, and you, more comfortable when they don't have to come and ask you for some shampoo because they forgot theirs.

N⁰ 54

ORGANIZING THE BATH

Keeping the bathroom well organized and clean can make my day start out so much better! Now if only the bathroom cleaned itself . . . We can dream right? Here are helpful tools to limit the mess in your bathroom getaway:

❦ **Drawer organizers.** Keep those drawers organized with simple organizers you can find at many stores. Made of canvas or plastic or wood, they will change the way your drawers work for you and keep all your small items organized and orderly.

❦ **Baskets.** Baskets are great for in the cupboards or even on the wall or on the floor. Use a separate one for each storage need: toilet paper, hair tools, makeup, cleaning supplies, and more.

❦ **Hooks.** Hang it all up! From robes to towels to tomorrow's outfit. Keeping things off the counters will keep the space tidy and make it somewhere you can unwind both morning and night for more peaceful days.

No 55 BATH-HAPPY PLANTS

If you are like me, you love to have plants in every room. After all, greenery brings every space to life and brings so much joy in the process. The bathroom might not be the first place you think of to grow and enjoy greenery, but it actually offers a great home for some humidity-loving plants. In return, the plants give life and beauty to a sometimes-stark room.

When it comes to the bathroom, lighting is usually low, but there are certain plants that love a little light, high humidity, and the warmth the bathroom provides from hot tubs and steamy showers. Here are a few plants that love to live in the bath:

1. Golden Pothos
2. Tillandsias
3. Spider plant
4. Snake plant
5. Tropical pitcher plant

Along with these five plants, succulents tend to do really well in these climates too. Adding any of these plants in a pretty pot can make your bathroom feel like a spa and might be the simplest way to add décor to your space. An added bonus? There is water nearby for your plant babies to drink, and being near a steamy shower will always make them happy!

TOWELS, ROBES, AND SLIPPERS

Hooks in the bathroom seem like an obvious addition, but what about what you hang on those hooks? I have to admit I'm a big cozy-towel snob, and I like my towels extra fluffy and big enough to wrap around me when I step out of the shower. Having a fluffy towel, a big robe, and some cozy slippers ready and waiting after you shower will turn the bathroom from just a regular room into a cozy retreat. And it can do the same in the guest bath for your visitors too!

Here's a tip: You know that not-so-special flannel robe and slippers that you use to muck into the yard when you're walking the dog in the morning? Let's relegate those to dog-walking time and have a luxuriously fluffy robe and slippers that you reserve for pampering time.

Thankfully, soft-and-fluffy pampering doesn't have to be as expensive as a spa trip. Here's my tip: keep it all white.

That way you can use different textures and styles of towels and take advantage of seasonal sales to stock up. When they're all white, they can live happily together in baskets and on shelves. And they'll always match any all-white robes and slippers. Clean, fresh, and consistently cozy.

DIY:

FACE MASK

Sometimes "cozy" is not what a space looks like, but what comforting moments happen there. So it is with pampering my skin in my bath. Over the years I have really grown to love using a face mask once a week to unwind. I've tried many types, but my favorites are the natural, homemade ones. I feel like my face responds to natural products so much better, and I don't have to stress about what ingredients I might be putting on my skin. Plus, natural items such as honey are so beneficial for your skin that you will glow from within when you use them. Here is one of my favorite DIY face masks that I use weekly. Even better, it has only three simple ingredients!

INGREDIENTS:

1 teaspoon honey—moisturizes, has antibacterial qualities for clearing blemishes, and includes antioxidants for anti-aging

1 teaspoon cinnamon—cures acne and blemishes, soothes dry skin, and alleviates fine lines

1 teaspoon nutmeg—heals scars and exfoliates

① Combine all ingredients in a small bowl.

② Use damp fingers to spread the mixture on your face, avoiding hair and sensitive eye area.

③ Leave on for twenty minutes, and then rinse thoroughly with warm water. Pat to dry.

N<u>o</u> 58   LAVENDER BATH SALTS

If you are a bath person, I highly recommend using bath salts. Epsom salts are known to help with sore muscles and cramps, but the combination with lavender and hot water can be very relaxing and turn a normal bath into a wonderful experience. After a day of work out on the farm, I love unwinding in a hot bath while I read a book and warm up my bones from the cold Michigan weather.

As a beautiful reminder to soak yourself often, mix dried lavender and Epsom salts into a pretty glass jar. Keep it near your tub, ready to scoop some into your bath when you need to unwind. You can also try adding different essential oils for your preferences and needs. The scents and the salts and the water and the warmth—they all combine to do wonders for your tired self. It's a lovely bit of self-care that your body and soul will thank you for.

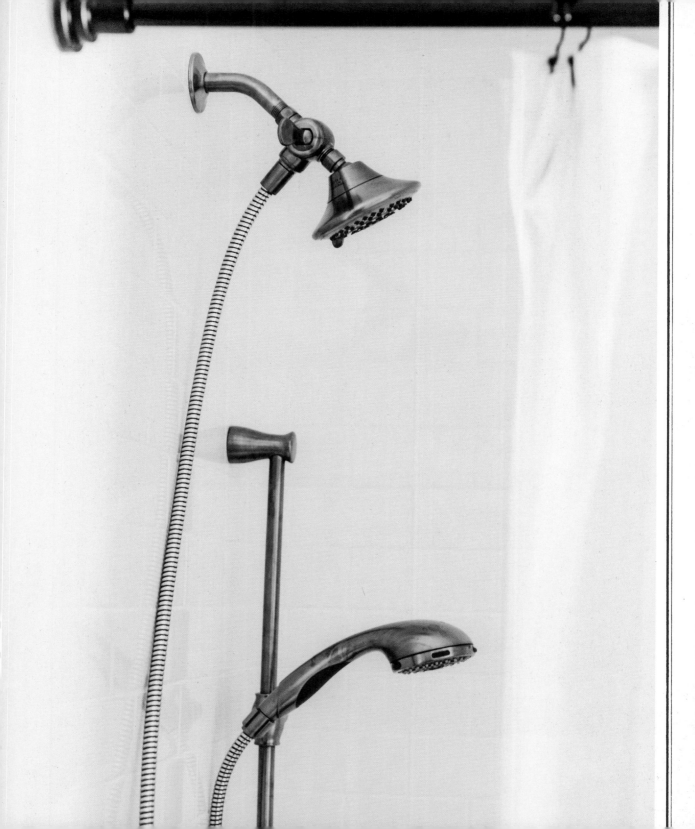

Nº 59

VINTAGE CLOCK

A clock in the bathroom might be the last thing you think about, but hear me out because it can comfort you more than you know. Picture a pretty vintage clock hanging on the wall, quietly reminding you of the right time (no technology needed). Not having to check my phone or run out of the room to check the time is a convenience I didn't know I needed. I'm not always known to be on time, which can be stressful, but a small addition like this keeps my stress down and keeps me on a perfect routine every morning.

DIY:

TUB TRAY

Is there anything better than soaking in a hot tub after a long day? Why not allow yourself to stay in the bubbles a little longer with a tray that makes soaking

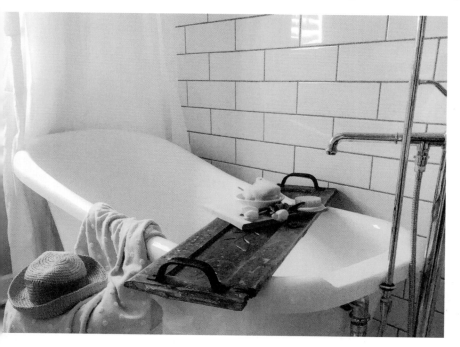

more convenient? A tub tray is a great way to let yourself relax while you soak since you'll have a convenient place to set a book or magazine and a cup of tea or your favorite beverage. So why not make your own tub tray? Visit LizMarieBlog.com/cozywhitecottagebook for step-by-step instructions. All you need is some wood, wood glue, and shellac. Grab some wood and cut it to the width of your tub from outside edge to outside edge. If your tub is off the wall, you can choose to have some overhang. Cut some pieces for the "legs" of the tray so it can slide side to side, and attach the legs with wood glue. Shellac the tray to keep it waterproof, and voila! You have your own bath tray to make your soak in the tub a little cozier.

No 61
DAILY SELF-CARE RITUALS

Life can get pretty stressful, and creating nighttime and morning rituals has been such a lifesaver for me. They allow me to unwind from a long day and to start the day fresh and revived. Here are a few steps to consider including in your own ritual:

- ⚜ A comforting skincare routine
- ⚜ Peaceful music
- ⚜ A candle burning
- ⚜ A hot, scented bath
- ⚜ Time for meditation or prayer
- ⚜ A few minutes reading or journaling
- ⚜ No technology

All of these could either prepare your mind for sleep or to start the day quietly.

Having a clean, organized, cozy bathroom truly helps make the daily self-care ritual more effective. So feel encouraged to spend a little time making your bathroom retreat-worthy and developing rituals you look forward to. I find that when I take time to renew myself, my day seems to run better and my mind is less hectic. Peaceful mornings and soothing nighttimes are perfect bookends to our cozy days.

CREATE

OFFICE & CRAFT ROOM

A cozy place to dream big dreams

OFFICE & CRAFT ROOM

The office. The room where dreams are often born, hard work brings them to fruition, and the daydreaming pays off in the end. We all have different goals, aspirations, and steps we want to take to live our cozy lives. For me? The office is a place that's functional enough for me to work on my dreams with few distractions yet beautiful enough to inspire me as soon as I walk through the doors. Welcome to the room of daydreams.

N⁰ 62 DIFFERENT PURPOSES

Home offices aren't always as "officey" as they once were. They are not only spaces for business but spaces for creating, a place to write, make, type, read, dream, create, and so much more.

Our office is where many of our dreams that eventually came to fruition, like this book, all started. These walls have seen many days of deep thoughts, failed projects, tons of tears, lots of creative gatherings, and countless late nights of hard work. They saw the very start and inner makings of our business, home plans, and farm life. This room is the heart of everything we do for work from our shop, The Found Cottage, to the farm, White Cottage Farm, and to my blog, LizMarieBlog.com, so it has been a work of love to make it a functional space for us to nurture our calling in life.

What job does your cozy home office need to do? For some people, the office is for writing a novel. For others it's for researching family ancestry, and for some, like us, the office serves many purposes at different times. Once you determine the purposes of your office space, you're well on your way to creating a cozy and functional office.

№ 63 OFFICE FUNCTION

Our office hasn't always nurtured our business. Far from it, actually. It wasn't until Jose and I really took stock of how we needed the space to work for us that the office started working for us. You can do the same.

To make your office functional and to keep you on a productive path, try creating workstations. I've never been voted the most likely to be productive, but I've found that workstations in my office allow me to leave everything else at the door when I come in to create. This isn't science, trust me (if it were, I wouldn't be doing it), but it's just simple and it works.

In my space, I have a table workstation where all my crafts and DIYs get done, a computer desk where much of my typing and writing happens, and a seating area where a lot of conversations and day-dreaming happens with Jose. I find that having organized workstations and tons of storage keeps me on task as I'm navigating through my workday.

We required quite a large office because of working from home and needing our home office to do a lot for us. But not everyone has the same needs. Some people don't need more than a simple table in the living room with a computer and a comfy chair to knock out some schoolwork or pay bills. Others may just have the corner of a den with a recliner and a plastic tub sitting next to it full of yarn to take care of their knitting while they watch TV. You know who had that? The classiest woman I know, the reason I'm sitting here writing this book, my grandma. She's the perfect example of how creative work and places to do it will look different for each of us. Make sure your work space is working hard to make your efforts and dreams all they can be.

№ 64 LAMPS

Lighting is a huge cozy factor. I'm talking HUGE. And when it comes to lighting, lamps are cozy 101. The glow from a lamp can induce so many feelings—from providing warmth as well as a sense of safety and calm.

A lamp on a table in a little reading corner can be so enticing, urging you to grab a book and a throw blanket to snuggle up for a night in. Even when overhead lighting is in a room, I add lamps to most spaces—from the kitchen to the living room, the entryway to the office, and beyond. And if you want pieces that pull double duty, hardworking lamps don't just add light. They also add texture, color, and height to a vignette.

N° 65 CHOOSING THE RIGHT LIGHT BULB

Choosing the right light bulb is very, very serious business when achieving a cozy space. You can have everything perfectly in place, from the right throw to the perfect wall décor, but you'll quickly fall short if you're lighting with a cool blue-toned light. Without diving way into the theory of lighting and the Kelvin scale, I suggest you look for bulbs with warm tones rather than cooler tones. Think of Christmastime, warming up next to a fireplace, that kind of warmth. Blue lights are described as institutional lighting, very white blue-toned lighting that makes you feel like you are in a doctor's office or laboratory, all anti-cozy spaces. Instead, I always go with soft white bulbs throughout the entire house. That's the cozy way to light.

N° 66 STORING AND DECLUTTERING HOME DECOR

One question I'm asked the most is, "Where do you store all of your extra home decor?" I've come up with a system that works in our home. Although we live in a fixer-upper and our house isn't the most organized because every room is unfinished, it's a system nonetheless. My secret? Don't keep it unless you love it. That concept has been life changing.

I used to keep a piece of home décor even if it was something I didn't love because I figured I might love it later. Although that could be true, it probably isn't going to happen often, and I have yet to regret being rid of less-than-loved items. The things I do keep but aren't in use are stored in one closet of our farmhouse, and I go through those shelves periodically to get rid of things so that I'm not overwhelmed. The key is to minimize the number of items you store, find a great spot like a closet or attic to keep it all organized, and know what you have.

So what do you do with all the décor that no longer has a home? First, decide if you want to reuse it in another part of your home. For instance, a dresser I'm thinking of getting rid of in our master bedroom might make a great buffet in our entryway.

If you can't reuse a piece elsewhere in your home, there are several great options for passing it on. First ask friends and family if they would like it. This one is my favorite ways to get rid of home décor because it's fun to be able to see the items being loved in other homes.

If no one I know wants to take an item off my hands, I move on to the next option: selling. Placing an item for sale in an online marketplace is a great way to declutter and get rid of unwanted items in your home.

The extra money can be used for new items to freshen up your spaces.

If you're ready to declutter but don't want to take the extra steps needed to sell online, consider donating the items. Call your local donation center to see what items they accept or what might be needed by charities in your areas; you can de-hoard and give back at the same time!

TEN-MINUTE COZY CHALLENGE

Here's a quick tip to get your space looking perfect: If you are stuck on a room or getting frustrated with a design in your home, set a timer each day for a 10-minute cozy challenge. Spend those ten minutes tinkering on a particular vignette or space. When the timer sounds, you're finished until the next day.

Too often we wait until we have a huge block of time or the right inspiration to tackle a design challenge, which can be overwhelming. Instead, take it little by little by walking away and coming back. You will be more refreshed and relaxed, and the happy results will soon show in the design.

DIY:

GALLERY WALL

Oh, the infamous gallery wall. The monumental focal point to a space that marries home décor and expressive art. I use gallery walls to display items that have meaning to me to better define our house. I like to think of it as a living mood board that gives a glimpse of what you can expect to see in the rest of the home.

Needless to say, gallery walls can come in all shapes and sizes, and they don't have to be restricted to framed photos. I've found that vintage finds can add beautiful textures such as signs, plates, paint brushes, and of course picture frames.

No matter what my gallery wall looks like, I constantly get asked if I have any tips on how to hang it. I have two methods, and one includes a lot of guessing

and unnecessary nail holes, so let's skip that way.

The *best* way to hang the gallery wall, with minimal damage to the wall, is to purchase brown builder's paper from the local hardware store. Gather the pieces you want to hang, trace them onto the builder's paper, and cut out to create a rough silhouette of each piece. Then use painter's tape to arrange these templates on the wall. This allows for you to step back and look at the gallery wall as a whole, rearranging items before setting the first nail or screw in place. Be mindful of spacing between objects; it's safe to keep the gaps as consistent as possible, not allowing too much space as it can disrupt the vibe and ambiance of the gallery wall.

No 69

FINDING JOY IN IT ALL

I hope you are sitting down somewhere while you are reading this. I hope it's cozy, I hope you are content, and I hope you are ready for the questions I'm about to ask. Look around you. Does everything in your home bring you joy? Does it help or benefit you and your family members? Or does it cause chaos and annoyance while contributing to clutter and mess? I know, that was a lot of questions, but they are so important to ask yourself as you assess your cozy home.

I may not be able to shed much wisdom from my thirty years of living, but I do know one thing from experience: Stuff causes stress. More stuff brings on more stress. More stuff doesn't mean more joy. Joy is loving everything that surrounds you and cozy is finding joy in everything and everyone in your home.

The process of decluttering is simple, but let me share a few tips that have helped me feel lighter, cozier, and happier in our home.

1. Do you need the item to assist your family for your daily needs? Does the item provide your home with joy from an assistance standpoint?
2. Do you love the item? Does the item give you joy when you look at it or use it? No? Toss it, donate it, or sell it.
3. Could a simple change make the item better? Could you paint the item, add something to the item, or move the item to a different room to make you love it more?

Those are questions I've asked myself as I've walked our entire home, from closets to bedrooms to our living quarters to our kitchen, and I can't believe what a weight it has taken off of me to rid our home of unwanted and unloved items. It has truly made our home cozier to have around only items that we love. Learning to find joy in it all is one of the biggest steps to making your home the coziest it can be.

It's funny how we can look at someone else's life or lifestyle and wish our spaces could be like theirs, but we forget we have the power to make changes to our own lives and spaces. It doesn't have to cost a lot of money if you don't want it to, maybe a can of paint here or a DIY project there. Just baby steps.

A little list of dreams and desires for our spaces is a great place to start. For many things in life, from our fertility journey to redesigning a room, I have grabbed my journal and made lists of what I desired to do to every space to make them cozy for our family and guests. Many of the things get put on the "future wish list" because of budget and time, but it's a start, and I'm a firm believer that writing your little and big dreams down is just the first step in bringing them to life. Here is a little list I made for our office even before it was something I talked to Jose about. My dream was to turn our dining room into an office for us. That dream came true this year, which was really exciting, but it all started with a simple list that looked something like this:

- Build an entire wall of built-ins
- Get a library ladder
- Build a desk for the center of the room
- Find antique lighting
- Add a rug

🌱 Find cozy desk chairs

🌱 Create a bar cart (perfect for coffee and cocoa!)

🌱 Display antique collections

🌱 Create office organization in cupboards

🌱 Paint walls a darker color

What about you? Think of a dream (or two), and try making a little list to bring it to life.

COLOR INSPIRATION

I often get asked why we stick to a very neutral wall color, from white to warm beiges, all a nod to the classic farmhouse style that uses a neutral painted base. It's a great question because there truly are so many wonderful paint colors. I'm so inspired by spaces with colorful walls, and once in a while I'll step out of a neutral wall color, but I do so love how a neutral wall gives us a clean palette and allows us to change our décor and styles effortlessly.

But you know what? If you want to spice it up, natural doesn't have to mean white, beige, or greige. A neutral can be anything deep and earthy. One of my biggest inspirations for décor is nature. Walks around the farm offer many palettes and décor ideas in our home. We can get inspired by the blues, greens, golds, and reds of nature and use that as a jumping-off point for our rooms. So take a nice long walk today—whether it's in the city, by a river, or around your farm—and look all around you, because

you're sure to find the color palette that inspires you.

GROW

— GARDEN —

A cozy place for beauty to bloom

GARDEN

Our first year in the garden, we were driven by the basics—fencing in a space, turning over the dirt, and quickly planting before we got too far into the season. There wasn't much cozy to be had. By the second year, I had learned a bit and was able to add some style and structure to the garden, creating an outdoor haven of sorts. But I also learned that this plot of land still has much to teach me.

The garden is one part of our homes that gives back, offering us produce, petals, and plenty of lessons in patience. I realize now that I'm not only growing a cozy garden; I'm growing a gardener as well, year by year and season by season.

GARDEN ENTRANCE

Cottage style can be added to the garden right at the entrance. A fun gate can be created from old doors, windows, or architectural structures from flea markets or antique shops. Along each side of the entrance, there are ways to add a look of French country cottage with running and climbing plants, or simple and cozy with some antique decor.

Our garden is in its infancy, but we have planted wisteria and hydrangeas, hoping to one day not know what's on the other side of the fence until you walk in. I imagine a living wall filled with vibrant greens and pops of hydrangea petals along the front face of the garden. Doesn't that sound lovely?

No 73

GARDEN STRUCTURES

I've recently noticed that a garden is so much more when it has a structure. I say structure, because it doesn't have to be a greenhouse, a shed, or anything too elaborate. It might be as simple as a trellis or arbor. Imagine walking into a garden with all its lovely bounty growing up from the ground. Now, imagine walking into that same foliage-filled garden, but your eye now travels to a lovely structure with ivy growing on the side of it, and then you get drawn into the garden chair that is by that structure, and it invites you in to come sit and look out onto the foliage.

Maybe structures just make a garden cozier. They can pull your eye up and lead you to the perfect cozy spot where the garden turns from just a place of beautiful work to a place of leisure and rest.

GARDEN TOOLS FOR BEGINNERS

It's no secret I love the garden. I'm a newer plant lady, not a pro—barely an amateur—but I am learning the ropes on how to keep plants alive and what you need to keep them healthy.

Gardening can be overwhelming for a beginner! You don't need to overwhelm yourself with unnecessary tools. Start with a few basics.

- ⚜ A basic gardening book; I love *Floret Farm's Cut Flower Garden* by Erin Benzakein
- ⚜ Garden boots
- ⚜ Garden gloves
- ⚜ A small-spout watering can
- ⚜ Hand trowel and garden fork
- ⚜ Plant markers (trust me, you will forget what you planted!)

№ 75

SHEDS

Did you ever have or want a playhouse in your backyard when you were little? I always wanted one of my very own where I could read and daydream and pretend I was grown up. Well, I'm all adult now, and I finally (finally!) got my playhouse—in the form of a garden shed! As a full-fledged grown-up, it's my favorite kind of backyard play.

Sheds can be purchased or built; regardless they can be styled—outside and in! This styling is what makes them more than just a storage space for your garden tools or seasonal items you don't need for a few months. Landscape around the front and create a path leading to the shed. Throw some flower boxes near the entrance or under the windows if it has them. You could also style the inside of the shed. When you're in the garden, leave the door open to be another indoor/outdoor space where you can sit to appreciate your garden, sip some lemonade, and get away from the sun. No matter your age, reading and daydreaming are still fully welcome.

A SHADY SPOT TO LAND

Is it weird that I forget that the coziest place to relax is under a shady tree in my yard? I grab a chair and carry it over to my favorite tree by the barn. I bring along a good book, my laptop, my phone, or just

a mug of something yummy and my dog. And I sit. The breeze moves my hair and the sun kisses my skin as the branches sway to reveal little peeks of the sunshine. When I'm out there, I remember that these shady outdoor spots are perfect frames for both simple moments of reflection and everyday working and writing tasks that are much easier to tackle with some fresh outdoor air.

Let me tell you a little secret . . . I'm actually outside sitting on a vintage lawn chair with my feet in the grass, the dogs by my side, and the sun on my feet as I type this. I was sitting here thinking of all things cozy, and I quickly was reminded how peaceful it is to enjoy nature while doing something I love. The view doesn't get much better than this, and it offers a treat for my senses and my soul. The smells, the sounds, the breezes, the sunlight—I can't help but smile as I take it all in. And you know what? I always feel closer to God when I'm out here in all this goodness He's made. I'm reminded that He values peace and He gave us beauty to fill us up.

I highly recommend pulling a chair or blanket, or just yourself, to a shady spot outside. Maybe like me you'll learn that cozy spots in the shade are not only a place for our bodies to land, but a place for our souls to rest as well.

If you're a plant lady like I am, nothing could be more fun and functional than a potting bench! Gardening work can be messy, and a potting bench is a cuter and more convenient space to pot plants, contain the mess, and organize and store tools.

For a simple DIY potting bench, I took an old table and a small shelf and attached the two pieces with L brackets. You also could easily make shelves to attach to an existing table; see LizMarieBlog.com/cozy-whitecottagebook for specific instructions.

N.º 78
OUTDOOR LIVING ROOM

Have you ever wanted to expand the square footage of your home? Did you know there is a way to quickly make your home feel instantly bigger by using the items you already have or with a small budget. How, you ask? Make your outdoor area part of your living space! Whether you have a patio, a deck, a yard, a balcony, or an alleyway, you can turn that square footage into a functional and comfy living space.

Imagine a living room outside, without the four walls but with the key pieces similar to those that make your indoor gathering areas inviting: a soft outdoor sofa, a table to prop your feet on, patio lights above you, and an outdoor rug below your feet. You can easily pick up a book, walk out the door, and enter into this cozy area as if it's just another room in your home. Now you instantly feel like you have more room to roam with just some simple updates outside.

In each home that we have lived in, we have made it a priority to make outdoor living spaces, and it's been one of the best decisions. There is something about being outside (with a few creature comforts from inside) that just inspires you to kick back and relax while laughing with family and friends. Here in Michigan our summers are short, so we have to make each day count. Having a comfy outdoor space lets us take advantage of warm nights and cool breezes; I highly recommend creating an under-the-stars living room for you and your family to enjoy—redefine cozy outside the four walls of home.

THE BALANCE OF PEACE AND HAPPINESS

I was at lunch recently with a friend, and I asked him what he thought cozy was. He answered that to him it's the perfect balance of peace and happiness. In my head, I thought that sounded wonderful, but I wondered what that was.

Well, as I walked down my stairs one morning after a restful night's sleep, I understood. I suddenly felt an inner coziness I hadn't felt in quite a while—the balance of peace and happiness. Was it from something big and groundbreaking? No. As I was walking down those stairs, I looked out onto the farm and I saw all the hard work we had done in the yard that week. Though my back still hurt, seeing the sun light up the clean farmyard put a smile on my face. As I continued looking out the window from the stairway, I saw the sheep happily eating away and the bee boxes buzzing. Downstairs I saw a clean house after a long week of taking the time for cleaning and organizing, even though it

wasn't something I had wanted to do at the time. And on the table was a Polaroid photo I took the night before of family hanging out in our front living room.

It dawned on me. This was cozy. That perfect balance of happiness and peace. Those two things don't always come easily. In fact, most of the time it's a lot of hard work, but every single fiber of my body was so thankful for all the hard work I had put in that week to reach these moments of cozy.

We can't control everything in our lives, so you may be rolling your eyes when I say you have to find the balance of peace and happiness, but trust me, I get it. Between our hectic schedules with the farm, the store, work, and many other things, my brain is usually going a mile a minute. It's hard to find peace some days, but I've discovered that when we take care of the things we can control—like ridding our homes of junk, keeping a tidy home,

doing our chores even when it's the last thing we want to do—we can wake up with that peace and that happiness because those things we can't control don't seem so large or daunting anymore. Being cozy is truly a gift worth working for.

PLAY

— MEDIA & PLAYROOM —

*A cozy place to make
memories together*

MEDIA & PLAYROOM

Playrooms and kids' corners might induce images of messy piles of germ-covered toys or a room in your home that you always hide by shutting the door when anyone comes to visit. But I'm here to hopefully help you give a new perspective on the playroom.

What if we treated the playroom like it was the birthplace of our child's hopes, dreams, and talents? What if we gave our little ones a space to thrive in, to discover, and to become their own little person? What if we looked at their little messes through nostalgic eyes, celebrating that they are healthy, happy, and developing in our cozy homes? What if we created their own little nook in our homes—whether it's a large and plush playroom, a little desk in the kitchen, or a magical corner of the living room—designated for them to get lost in their imaginations? When they have their own space, it gives them the freedom to be kids and hopefully makes cleaning for you a tad easier. Win-win, right? Creating a space for littles (and bigs) to dream can be one of the greatest ways to create a cozy home.

№ 80 INTERACTIVE COLLECTIONS

One of my fondest childhood memories is being at my grandma's home and actually playing with her antique collections of figurines, dolls, and, of course, her cherished vintage buttons. Her large collection of buttons would keep me busy for hours—sorting, designing, and dreaming with those little antique beauties.

By letting me play with her collection, my grandma gifted me forever memories and inspired the adult me to want everything in our home to be touchable, useable, and beautiful. I actually have my own button collection started, and I look forward to the day my kids are able to enjoy the simple pleasure of sorting buttons and making cozy memories while playing with them on the floor.

From a young age, I appreciated the charm all antiques held, but my favorite antiques have always been ones I could touch and interact with. Pretty and fragile pieces are nice, but the ones you can use daily like antique stoneware plates for dinner and button collections for play and DIY are the best. Coming into your home or someone else's home and feeling like you can't touch anything for fear of breaking it is not cozy. Being able to use all your senses, including touch, allows you to live in every space of your home.

Interactive collections are a great way to decorate while sharing your passions, style, and memories with others. . . . a sweet encouragement for the child in us all to stay alive and well.

N⁰ 81

CHALKBOARDS

Chalkboards aren't just for the classroom anymore. They now work all over the home, with that chalky black or green surface adding tons of old-school texture and depth. Our dining room is a very neutral white space that is super cozy, but when we added an oversize chalkboard above one of our antique rolling carts, it added an instant pop of depth and now acts as super-affordable, large-scale art. Whether we are drawing on it with chalk or layering a banner or piece of art over it, the chalkboard is a unique way to fill a large wall.

Needing a fun place to add a chalkboard? Try adding one in a playroom or office, where it can be both pretty and functional. Use it for hand-lettering or penmanship practice for the kids or for list making for the grown-ups. Do you have a large wall you need to fill? DIY a chalkboard by painting a piece of plywood with some chalkboard paint from your local hardware or craft store. Build a simple frame for it using scrap wood cut at 45-degree angles (see my blog for a full DIY at LizMarieBlog.com/cozywhitecottagebook).

And feel free to move your chalkboards from room to room as the seasons or family activities change. A mudroom chalkboard is a great place to track that week's soccer schedule in the spring, but during the holidays it can set up shop in the entryway to welcome party guests. In any room, the chalkboard is one decorative piece that earns its keep.

Sometimes form and function do not need to compromise. It's no secret that barn doors are a really easy way of adding character to your home without a major overhaul. Pull out the builder-grade door and throw up a custom-made barn door or vintage find from your latest picking adventure. I've hung barn doors throughout my home, but I still keep an eye out at markets for unique vintage doors, because it's a fast and fairly inexpensive way to change the look of a space when you're ready for a little refresh.

Doors play a really important role in our homes, but when you think about it, most interior doors are pretty nondescript. Close your eyes. Now try to picture what the doors in your house look like. What about your best friend's house or your mom's house? Most of the time specifics won't come to mind. But when you hang a barn door in your house, it's memorable.

It's distinct. It adds interest and age and uniqueness that visitors (and you!) will remember.

An ugly sofa. We've all had one. Okay, maybe *ugly* is harsh, but we've all had that one piece of furniture we don't love. It's a predicament. But did you know that simply throwing a quilt over the sofa can make a temporary slipcover? That's what I did when I wasn't in love with our sunroom sofa. My simple fix was a vintage quilt that was large enough to cover the whole sofa. I tucked the quilt all around it into the cushions to create a slipcover I was much happier with until I found a more permanent solution. I already had the quilt, so it took me five minutes, and I loved how it turned out.

When "don't wait" becomes your motto, look for simple fixes like this one. They may be temporary, but they can make you fall in love with your cozy space all the more quickly.

N<u>o</u> 84

EDIT YOUR SPACE

To create spaces I'm happy with, one of my biggest secrets is to edit. I am constantly editing in our home and in our store, but I'm not sure if I've ever talked about the process out loud before. Whether you're working on a small vignette in your home or doing a whole room overhaul, editing the space is the strongest way to check your foundation and ensure just the right amount of cozy.

What do I mean by *foundation*? Well, there are two phases to editing your space. The first is when you embark on a new project and edit the space by deciding what you want to keep or toss. Really look around and think of how you and your family will be living in the room; then only keep what is useful. When you empty the space you are working on, you can really get a fresh start on the vignette, and the final product will turn out so much better when the foundation is well cleaned and well thought out.

The second phase to editing? When you are done with your original plan in your space, whether it's an entire room or a vignette, take a step back and study the space. Live with the arrangement for a few hours or a day. Take a few photos and spend some time looking them over. With these steps, you will really see if something is off. Look for the balance. Ask yourself: *Is there equal weight on both sides? Is the scale appropriate for the wall? Is it too busy? What feels off?*

When you edit your space, you take out all the things you don't love about it, the things that don't work, and the pieces that just aren't useful. That doesn't mean that you take out too much. If you are like me, you love a little clutter, which might sound negative, but to me cozy isn't a stark space. I want pretty things to look at, I want little treasures around me that I collect, and I love the cozy element that art and collections can give a space. But sometimes I go

overboard. We are all guilty of doing too little or too much in a space and just living with it. That's where editing comes in.

When I start decorating a space, I always have an idea of a feeling, a look, or a vibe I'm going for. I know some people go in with an exact plan, but in our home I'm more of a figure-it-out-as-you-go kind of planner (unlike when I'm designing for others). I feel like in our home if I plan too much, the design is too stiff and doesn't give that cozy vibe that I love so much. I go in with a general idea, some items that I want to use, but I know that in the editing process so much can change. I highly recommend stopping along the decorating road to edit—it's a great trick of the trade!

№ 85 TIPS FOR EDITING

Take photos to see what looks "off." Example: Step back with your camera and take shots from several angles and distances. When you examine the pics, you might be amazed at what the camera saw that your eye did not.

- **Try new things.** Example: Do you have a centerpiece you are working on? Maybe take out the wood candlesticks and add a bowl of fruit to see if you like that better. Or maybe in a gallery wall swap out a cluster of three picture frames and try a large mirror in their spot. Try new things and edit to see if something works better and if you fall in love with it more.

- **Take something out.** Example: Maybe you don't need six frames above a sofa. Maybe just one large piece of art will look cleaner and more substantial for such a large space. Take out the six frames and replace with one larger item. Or maybe you don't need seven pumpkins in your centerpiece; take a few out, and maybe it will look cleaner and less cluttered.

- **Add life to the space.** Example: Not loving your coffee table? Add a plant, real or fake, to give that space some life. Sometimes all a vignette needs is a little life, and plants are the perfect finishing touch that is sometimes missing.

- **Live with it for a few days.** Example: When you are finished with a room refresh, live with it a few days and really dwell in the space to see if it functions well, if you feel like it's missing something, or if you need to make any changes for it to perform better. Truly living with the changes will tell you a whole lot about your new space.

N⁰ 86

A PLAYROOM FOR ALL AGES

What could be cuter than a child creating and dreaming at your farmhouse dining table? The correct answer is a child creating at a *mini* farmhouse dining table. Too often when we imagine a playroom, we tend to picture it filled with plastic children's furniture from a big box store. But Erin from CottonStem.com uses a different strategy, creating a space that encourages her kids to be little, all while keeping things beautiful.

Erin is a huge inspiration for someone like me who is starting a life with littles. She and I both embrace the idea of creating sophisticated children's spaces that are aesthetically pleasing and welcoming to everyone in the family. So although her mini farmhouse table is a perfect spot for her littles to create and dream, the kid-friendly room is also cohesive with the rest of her home.

With a few miniature-size pieces to make your kids comfy, a room where they can create and play doesn't have to be anything less (or more plastic) than your existing décor. And it can be a place where adults can be creative and playful as well. In a beautiful space like this, kids can still embrace being little—they'll just be doing it in style.

DIY:

LARGE ART

I can't be the only one who has searched high and low for the right-sized art with the right-sized frame for the right-sized space in our home. You can feel stuck to what big-box stores are offering and what you happen to find at your local antique and thrift shops, but why not make your own? Did you know that your local office-supply store or print shop will print out a photo of your choice in the size of your choice?

Recently I was determined to find just the right thing to cover up our TV in our front living room when we weren't watching it. I found a large antique frame while out and about picking, and I had a photo from our farm blown up to fit the frame. We hung it over our TV with an ingenious hanging system Jose created. (Read more about this DIY on the blog at LizMarieBlog. com!) You can create a large (or small) cozy piece of custom art simply by sending a photo to a print shop and getting a custom-size printed just for you and your space. What do you do with your print? Find a frame, have a frame made at your local craft shop, or DIY your own frame for your new custom photo!

If you don't have a photo in mind already, here are some ideas for your custom-size artwork:

- ❦ Take a close-up photo of a floral arrangement in your home.
- ❦ Find a landscape shot of your favorite place to visit.
- ❦ Get in really close and take a photo of an animal, pet, or child. Try a different angle.
- ❦ Consider a zoomed-in photo of a favorite toy—perfect for the playroom or a kids' bedroom.
- ❦ Enlarge an existing family photo (old black-and-white pics are great options!).

BONUS TIP: If you need help editing your photo, our photo presets will let you edit like a pro in one easy step. Find out more on our blog: LizMarieBlog.com.

N° 88

COZY GLOW

Candles are a great way to give your room a cozy glow, of course, but it's not always convenient to light a candle in certain spots, like on a shelf, high up, near plants, or in reach of kids and pets. My secret to getting that warm glow is with battery-powered twinkle lights! They are so cheap and can be safely used anywhere in your home to add a needed bit of sparkle.

I add twinkle lights in jars, on top of cabinets, in greenery, in cloches, on shelves, and so much more. You can find strands of battery-powered lights in many different sizes, shapes, colors, and styles. In the playroom, twinkle lights add a perfect ambiance to movie night or any night, making your home cozy all year round.

REST

— BEDROOM —

A cozy place to soothe your soul

BEDROOM

When you think about it, we spend more time in our bedrooms than in any other room of the house. It's where we do some of our most important work—sleeping, dreaming, and resting. A cozy bedroom makes this work easier, and nowhere else is cozy as welcome as here, snuggled in the middle of all things soft. It's the place for the more intimate side of cozy, where we typically welcome only our favorite people, the family pets, and the occasional cookies in bed.

The bedroom ends and begins most days of our lives, so why not make it a place where you can find the coziest rest ever? Bookend each day with the cozy it deserves.

HOW TO MAKE A BEDROOM SOOTHING

Our bedrooms should be soothing, a place to gather us in at night and comfort us. That looks different for everyone, but for me there are some simple steps I like to follow to make the bedroom as cozy and soothing as possible:

- ❧ **Clutter free is the way to be.** I like to keep our bedroom free of anything extra that I don't find useful or that doesn't bring peace to our space. Only bring beautiful things into the room.
- ❧ **Keep it tidy.** For me, keeping our bedroom tidy with the bed made and the space picked up brings me so much peace each night. (This is easier when there isn't clutter.) A clean room is a soothing escape from the messy world.
- ❧ **Choose quality.** This one I've learned as I left my twenties behind. Investing in a quality mattress, bedding, and pillows is worth it.
- ❧ **Limit technology.** And say no to blue light TV.
- ❧ **Keep a journal.** Before going to sleep at night, list three blessings from each day.

№ 90

WOOD APPLIQUÉS

Sometimes a new piece of furniture isn't in the budget or you just want to give an existing wood piece a little makeover. I have the simplest way to spice up a piece of furniture (besides painting), and it can make the transformation in mere minutes. The magical easy trick? Adding wood appliqués to furniture. Wood appliqués or ornamental wood pieces can be found at craft and hardware stores in so many different shapes and styles. They are easily glued to the front of a dresser, the top of a trunk, the sides of a table, and so much more. Instant satisfaction!

BASKET-O'-BLANKETS

We all don't run on the same temperature, that is for sure. One of my favorite things to have in sitting rooms around the home including the bedrooms is a large basket filled with quilts and pillows. Having the quilts easily accessible and ready to grab for you and everyone else makes the room comfortable no matter what temperature each person is running at. I put the basket in an accessible spot and usually fill it with cozy quilts of all different sizes and textures so everyone can pick their favorite. The best part?

A cozy basket filled with quilts is a great large piece of décor to fill a spot in your room. It instantly makes the space cozy!

№ 92

DOG BEDS

For us lucky ones who have a dog in the house, our furry friends already make the home ten times cozier. But I've found another way to add snugness to your home when you have a dog—dog beds. No longer the shabby pillows you are picturing in your head, dog beds have really stepped up their game in the past few years and have become customizable to fit your home's style. A dog bed made from vintage grain sack in a room adds a pouf of coziness that makes everyone feel more at home, especially the dogs. You can find amazing-looking dog beds that fit your décor at many different online retailers, including some amazing ones on Etsy!

N° 93

PERFECT READING CORNER ESSENTIALS

Sometimes our homes don't allow for us to have an entire room filled with cozy furniture and relaxing essentials where we can shut the door and close out the world to escape into a book or stitch our latest craft. No worries! A little corner is all you need to create a quiet nook perfect for a cozy hot chocolate snuggle session with a good book or a morning coffee devotional moment to start your day.

- ⚜ Let's start with a cozy base and lay down a small rug that fits in the corner of your room and defines your reading corner.
- ⚜ Pick your perfect chair or small settee. Is it a recliner, an antique chair, a deconstructed beauty, or a slipcovered oversized chair that fits two? Find the perfect seat that fits your home's aesthetic, but that also draws you to it for moments of relaxation when they are needed.

- ⚜ Find a small table or stool that you can use to either prop your feet up or use to set your cup of tea on.
- ⚜ Add some light, whether it's a lovely little table lamp or a floor lamp that works like task light for the work you will be doing.
- ⚜ Add your essentials: As a bonus keep your corner stocked with things that you will use there, whether it's a Bible or devotional, a pair of slippers, a log holder for the fireplace, a book, a candle, or the latest craft you are working on.

I have been forever inspired by the little reading corners in my grandma's home growing up. One in particular was in their sunroom where I would often find her sitting when I came to visit. Next to the chair was a rack of her latest design magazines, a side table with the telephone, and one of the coziest chairs I had ever sat in.

her reading corner. Oh my, if that reading corner could talk! I bet it holds a lot of family secrets that she was very good at keeping. But looking back, I love that she kept that phone in her reading corner because it was a place she could relax and truly listen to the person on the other side of the line. She would sit in her cozy chair and be the best listening ear I have ever known and offer some of the best advice I have ever heard. I was often the one on the other end of the phone line and I always pictured her in that reading corner while I talked about all my latest trials and triumphs. Those moments have inspired various reading corners in our home, because I think they can teach us a lot of life lessons we didn't even know we needed.

In fact, I still have that chair today in our farmhouse recovered in some new fabric. I remember her taking all her phone calls from our various family members and her friends in that corner. I sat on the sofa across from her, panning through the magazines listening to her on the phone in

HOW TO MAKE A COZY BED

What is the number-one focal point and most important piece in every bedroom? The bed. Whether you have a king, queen, twin, four-poster, metal farmhouse, or simple platform with a mattress, we must make that bed cozy. We spend so much of our lives sleeping, so why not make that bed of ours as comfortable as we can while having it look its best? I have a few tips to make the perfect cozy bed that will surely help you fall in love with sleeping all over again.

- **Choose a good mattress.** I know it's not always in the budget, but if you don't love your mattress, I highly recommend budgeting for one when possible. You have heard it before: a good mattress makes a world of difference. I'm a firm-mattress girl myself and didn't know that until I tested and purchased a new one. I can't tell you how much it changed my sleeping habits and the way my body felt in the morning. It's a good base to your best cozy bed.

- **Overstuff that duvet cover.** If you choose to use a duvet cover, fill it up! You can size up on the down-filled duvet insert or you can double up on the inserts to really fill that cover to its fullest and make the entire bed fluffier.

- **Get some large pillows.** I'm a huge fan of overstuffed pillows everywhere in the home, but especially the bedroom. I recommend sizing up on your throw-pillow inserts one size to get that perfect overstuffed pillow look. A bed with too-small pillows can look crowded and not that cozy, so go big! Grab some Euro-sham size throw pillows, and you will be all set.

- **Load up on layers.** Layer your bedding to get a fuller and cozier look to your bed. Your favorite sheets with a lovely quilt on top and an overstuffed duvet folded at the end make the bed look tempting at all times of the day. When you make the bed, roll back the blankets to show off your luxe layers and reveal the perfect decadent look you see in all the department stores. Then layer your pillows by putting your regular pillows behind some large stuffed Euro shams.

A well-made bed is perfect for sinking in to at the end of the day, although lingering there at the beginning of the day is encouraged as well! Now your bedroom's focal point can be your cozy point too, welcoming you to a place of rest.

LAYER PILLOWS

Layering pillows on a sofa or bed is kind of a simple science. Here is the way I like to break it down when making it cozy with pillows.

Start with two anchor pillows that are larger and match each other. Place these anchors on each side of the sofa. From there you want to work your way in by mixing some patterns. You don't want it to look too curated, so mixing the patterns makes it feel more relaxed and effortless.

Mixing patterns is fail proof; the secret is to keep it all in the same color scheme. For example, let's keep it really simple and go with the classic black and white. You could have two large white pillows as your anchor on each end of the sofa, next put two black-and-white stripe pillows, and then mix it up with a smaller black-and-white pattern and maybe a black-and-white fringe pillow

for some interest. That's the fail-proof way, but of course you can go outside the lines and mix colors and more patterns if you are feeling that vibe. Another option is to use an all-neutral base and pop on an accent pillow that is a unique color or shape.

TIP: Pillows look so much more expensive when they are full and not slouchy, so always size up on the inserts. For example, if you have a 22-inch pillow cover, get a 24-inch insert. I also recommend using a down-filled insert if possible because it will make your pillows more luxurious, and they will keep their shape better over time.

A favorite DIY project that Jose and I have done is a fireplace mantle for the master bedroom. It had long been our dream to have a bedroom fireplace in our 1800s farmhouse, especially during the cold winters here in the Mitten State, and we finally took it upon ourselves to add this cozy feature. See my blog at LizMarieBlog.com/cozywhitecottagebook for instructions.

We started with an electric fireplace insert we bought from Amazon. We built the framework for the fireplace, then added trim. Jose created some custom corbels to support a mantle ledge, giving the new build some old character and vintage detail.

The cool feature that Jose added is two doors to hide our TV. The tapestry might seem in the way, but it has grommets at the top. To open, we simply take the grommet off one of the screws on the door to open the doors, and place the grommet back on the screw when we shut the door again. Super simple!

No 97
INVEST IN SLEEPWEAR

Some lessons we only learn as we get older—like how to do your taxes and make your own bread. But why is it that we will spend money going out to eat and spoiling others in our lives, but we won't invest in great sleepwear? Let's all do this together today. . . . Let's go into our pajama drawer and pull out those uncomfortable, holey pajama bottoms and paint-stained T-shirts. Instead, let's invest (and it doesn't even have to be a lot) in some cozy loungewear that we can look and feel good in.

There is something about knowing I can go home and change into something so comfortable that literally relaxes me instantly. Maybe for you that *is* a paint-stained T-shirt

and some holey pajama bottoms. But I would suggest that lounging and sleeping in extra-comfy, extra-pretty sleepwear makes everything seem better (even if you also wear it to walk the dog). You're not only investing in sleepwear, you're investing in rest. And that is worth every penny.

№ 98

THE LOW-TECH BEDROOM

Our lives get so hectic no matter what season of life we are in. From running around with kids for some to working all day to just keeping up with all the things that we have to keep up with. One way I've learned to cozy up our bedroom is to leave technology at the door and put my phone away an hour or two before bedtime. Not scrolling through Instagram and Facebook before bed has caused a huge shift in my ability to rest and turn my mind off so that I'm able to wake up in a good state of mind.

So how did I stick with the switch to leaving my phone at the bedroom door? It was quite simple. I gave that time to God. I had been struggling to find time for prayer and meditation before, but really it was because I wasn't making it a priority in my life. I've found that focusing on prayer and meditation before bed has truly been a huge step in self-care for my mind.

Our minds race all day with to-do lists, tasks, worries, and the floods of what others are doing, so to be able to turn that off at least an hour before bed so that we go to sleep with a clear mind is a luxury of a renewable resource called peace.

No. 99 LOVING YOUR LIVED-IN HOME

I hope you know that what truly makes your home cozy is actually letting it be lived in, letting it be a place where you and your loved ones can feel the floor with your bare feet and throw flour around the kitchen when you cook. Living without fear that your home is not perfect every step of the way and that it's not magazine (or book) worthy seven days a week is where it's at.

Our social media world makes us think that everyone else's homes are always pristine, but that's not the real world! Please believe this about those of us who love our cozy homes: we have throw pillows on the floor where our friends came over and piled on them while we played board games. We have paint swatches on the walls because we want to live with them for a few days to see what color we like best. And plenty of surfaces are covered with blankets, kids' artwork, toys, and so much more because we live to the fullest inside these walls . . . and you should too.

FINDING CONTENTMENT

Do you ever find yourself comparing your life to someone else's? What about your home? Well, you are not alone. We all fall to comparison, especially in this social-media-crazy culture we live in. Even though you are not alone, it doesn't mean it's just a feeling you have to settle for. The constant comparison and wishing for more can leave you in a place where you are no longer content with your home. Instead of being a haven, it becomes a constant reminder of what you are lacking and what is wrong with your space.

When we are more content with our homes, we start to realize that it's not about perfection, especially while living in a fixer-upper like Jose and I do. It's never going to be perfect! Just like life, it's all a process. My biggest lesson from living in a fixer-upper has been to enjoy each stage of the process, making it a cozy sanctuary for our family even if it means covering holes in the floor with boards and sweeping

sawdust to the other side of the room so we can walk through without getting dirty feet. When we first bought our old farmhouse, I found myself apologizing to guests and to people seeing shared photos online. I would say, "Sorry it looks like this. . . . We are making changes soon" or even calling our house ugly and downplaying this wonderful dream farm we had prayed for.

After many months of being exhausted from striving for daily perfection, I finally woke up one day and made it a point to stop apologizing. To stop longing for those days when our home would be finished and for my idea of what I wanted all of it to look like when it was done. If I'm not enjoying the process, am I really just wishing my life away striving for perfection and a perfect home? So instead, I'm enjoying the whole messy process, sawdust and all. I'm welcoming joy into every season of our home and making it an enjoyable experience for everyone. And I hope you

can do the same! I mean, we might as well make the process enjoyable. After all, isn't it the love we put into a home what really makes it beautiful? Let's try to be content along the way, with ourselves and with our homes. Every stage of life (and renovation) offers beauty, comfort, and coziness for us to find.

WHERE WE LOVE TO SHOP

Whether you're saving to splurge on a big piece, or you're working on a tight budget, we've discovered that cozy home items can be found everywhere from national chains to your favorite local antique store. Here are a few of our particular favorites:

Terrain

The Found Cottage

Anthropologie

HammMade Furniture

Pottery Barn

Farmhouse Frocks

Madewell

Etsy

Wallpaper Direct

Painted Fox Home

Serena & Lily

Cottonwood Shanty

Amazon

Ikea

Joss & Main

Barn Light Electric

McGee & Co

Antique Candle Co.

Bemz Slipcovers

Arhaus

Schoolhouse Electric

Honey Home Market, Etsy

World Market

Target

Walmart

Wayfair

ACKNOWLEDGMENTS

To Anna Vandenberg: Thank you so much for helping me bring this book to life. Our photoshoots together were not only fun but also inspiring. Thank you from the bottom of my heart for the hard work you put into this book. I could not have done it without you!

To Michelle (Burke) Freeman: Thank you so much for helping me bring my voice to this book. The amount of work that goes into a book with this many style tips and DIYs was harder than I could have ever imagined. You probably had the hardest job—keeping me on a schedule and on track—and I cannot thank you enough for helping me get to the end of this and present a book I can be proud of. Thank you, friend.

To Dawn and MacKenzie: I would not be here without either of you. I never thought the title *author* would be attached to my name. . . .

To Lisa VanDyke and Abby Hoppen-Albers: My business partners, aunt, and best friends. Thank you for being by my side throughout this journey. My attention may not have always been on The Found Cottage, but because of you I was able to juggle being a shop owner, blogger, and new momma. So much thanks to you both. Love you!

To all my fellow bloggers and creatives: My love and passion as a creative and designer truly flourish around other creatives. Words cannot express my gratitude for all my friends out there!

To the beautiful ladies who contributed photos of their cozy homes for this book: Erin Kern, www.cottonstem.com (pages 20, shelves; 27; 60, far right mantle; and 182). Sue

Vanderveen, www.fabricscoutstudio.com (pages 128, 130, 132, 136, 142, 144, 168, 171, 187, and 211). Lynzy Coughlin, www.lynzyandco.com (pages 123, 124, 131, 135, 184). Lauren McBride, www.laurenmcbrideblog.com (page 45). Kristi Bissell, www.thepickledrose.com (page 138). Thank you!

To all my favorite shops and vendors: Thank you for finding all the things. My love for antiques and unique pieces is so big . . . I am so happy to live in such a wide community that brings things from all over the nation.

To my readers: Thank you for joining us on this journey and on so many others. I could not have asked for a better community of people to share my ideas and stories with, and I'm grateful for all you've made possible.

To my neighbor and good friend, Diane Reiffer, and to our parents, John and Lynne DeBruin and Tom and Rose Busman: I love you all so much. Thank you for all of your support.

To my son! Cope, I started this book dreaming one day of having a little baby to share all these cozy spaces with and a reason to decorate a playroom. I am beyond myself that I am writing my last chapters holding you on my lap. You are more than your dad and I could have ever asked for. We love you, son, and I hope you are proud of your momma.

To Jose: For being my rock in all things and supporting my dreams since day one, even when they didn't make sense. For always making me feel totally loved and for telling me how inspiring I am daily. You inspire me with how selfless and giving you are. You are the best dad and the best husband, and Cope and I are lucky to have you.

And to God who makes all things possible: I give this book back to you because by your glory it was possible.

About the Author

LIZ MARIE GALVAN is a blogger, interior designer, and co-owner of the vintage home décor boutique The Found Cottage (TheFoundCottage.com). Each month hundreds of thousands of readers find design inspiration and DIY ideas at LizMarieBlog.com. Liz and her veteran husband, Jose, live on an 1800s farmhouse in Michigan with their son Copeland, their dogs, cats, sheep, and rams. Learn more about their farmhouse renovation at TheWhiteCottageFarm.com. Find Liz on Instagram @lizmariegalvan.

Liz has been featured in *Better Homes and Gardens*, *Country Living*, *Garden & Gun*, and *Coastal Living* magazines and has collaborated with Behr, Magnolia Home Paint, KILZ®, Home Depot, T.J. Maxx/HomeGoods, Home Depot, GMC, and HGTV.